R

MAY 1 9 2021

Magnolia Library

D0340991

ROCK FORCE

ALSO BY KEVIN MAURER

American Radical

Hunter Killer

No Hero

No Easy Day

Gentlemen Bastards

No Way Out

Lions of Kandahar

Hunting Che

Valleys of Death

ROCK FORCE

The American Paratroopers
Who Took Back Corregidor
and Exacted MacArthur's
Revenge on Japan

KEVIN MAURER

CALIBER

Dutton Caliber
AN IMPRINT OF PENGUIN RANDOM HOUSE LLC
www.penguinrandomhouse.com

Copyright © 2020 by Kevin Maurer
Penguin supports copyright. Copyright fuels creativity, encourages diverse voices,
promotes free speech, and creates a vibrant culture. Thank you for buying an
authorized edition of this book and for complying with copyright laws by not
reproducing, scanning, or distributing any part of it in any form without
permission. You are supporting writers and allowing Penguin to
continue to publish books for every reader.

DUTTON CALIBER and the D colophon are registered trademarks
of Penguin Random House LLC.

LIBRARY OF CONGRESS CATALOGING-IN-PUBLICATION DATA
has been applied for.

ISBN 9781524744762 (hardcover)
ISBN 9781524744786 (ebook)

Printed in the United States of America
1   3   5   7   9   10   8   6   4   2

BOOK DESIGN BY KATY RIEGEL

While the author has made every effort to provide accurate telephone numbers,
internet addresses, and other contact information at the time of publication, neither
the publisher nor the author assumes any responsibility for errors or for changes that
occur after publication. Further, the publisher does not have any control over and
does not assume any responsibility for author or third-party
websites or their content.

To the paratroopers of the 503rd Parachute Infantry

Regiment past, present, and future

Contents

Contents

Author's Note

THE WORDS "JAP" AND "NIP" are racial slurs used by American soldiers during World War II to describe the Japanese. Soldiers in every war use slurs to dehumanize the men they are trained to kill, but that doesn't excuse their use. Both words appear in this book in quotes only because it offers a factually accurate depiction of how the soldiers spoke in 1945 at the height of the Pacific war.

Intrinsically, Corregidor is but a barren, war-torn rock, hallowed, as so many places, by death and disaster. Yet it symbolizes within itself that priceless, deathless thing, the honor of a nation. Until we lift our flag from its dust, we stand unredeemed before mankind. Until we claim again the ghastly remnants of its last gaunt garrison, we can but stand humble supplicants before Almighty God. There lies our Holy Grail.

—GEN. DOUGLAS MACARTHUR,

May 1943

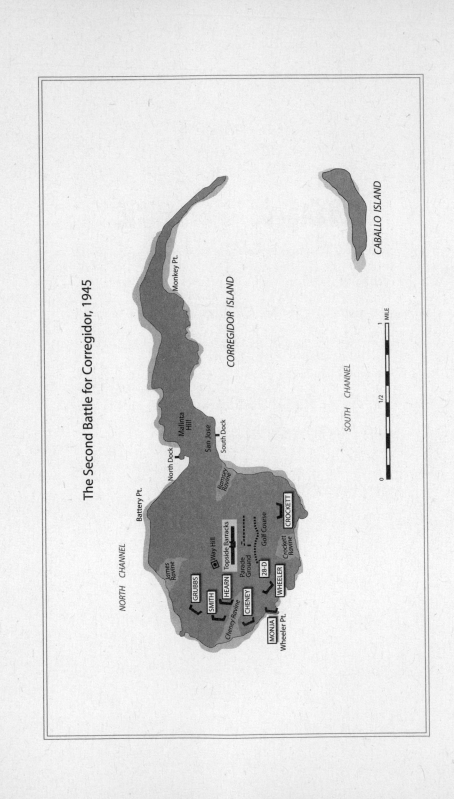

The Second Battle for Corregidor, 1945

NORTH CHANNEL

Battery Pt.

CORREGIDOR ISLAND

Monkey Pt.

North Dock

Malinta
Hill

San Jose

South Dock

James
Ravine

GRUBBS

Ramsey
Ravine

SMITH

Way Hill

Topside Barracks

HEARN

Cheney Ravine

CHENEY

Parade
Ground

28-D

Golf Course

MONJA

WHEELER

Crockett
Ravine

CROCKETT

Wheeler Pt.

SOUTH CHANNEL

CABALLO ISLAND

0   1/2   1
MILE

ROCK FORCE

The Rock

BEFORE IT WAS a fortress, Corregidor was a volcano.

Born below the waves of the Pacific Ocean, the island slowly rose, one violent eruption after another, before it finally broke the surface, rising toward the morning sun. Layer after layer it grew, until it towered hundreds of feet above the water. Over time, the eruptions slowed, and the volcano sank. The magma remaining in the open air cooled and hardened. Then the waves went to work, smashing the sharp volcanic rock into soil and sand, life took hold. Brush and vines rooted into the barren brown land, repainting it a vibrant green against the blue sea.

The Spanish realized the importance of the island in 1570, when they saw it for the first time as they sailed into Manila Bay. Towering out of the water, it stood 589 feet above the surface at its highest point, its high, imposing cliffs choking with vines and trees. Stretching slightly more than four miles, with a long, narrow, whiplike tail, it was only a little more than a mile wide at most, tapering off gradually to a tip that looked out over the expanse of the bay.

After claiming the Philippine archipelago, the Spanish set a lookout and cannons on the small mountain at the head of the island so soldiers could signal Manila's defenses of an approaching enemy fleet. Then came a lighthouse for ships sailing in from the South China Sea. A customs station and a small fishing village followed. Soon, all ships heading to Manila stopped at the island so officials could check their papers, earning the island its name: Corregidor, which means "magistrate" or "corrector" in Spanish.

It wasn't until US Navy Commodore George Dewey led his squadron into Manila Bay and occupied the Philippines in 1898 that the island finally grew into a fortress. Dewey's victory was part of the ten-week war between Spain and the United States, fought in both the Caribbean and the Pacific, and the American triumph signaled the end of the Spanish Empire and marked the United States' first steps onto the world stage. At war's end, US interests spanned the globe, stretching from Puerto Rico in the Caribbean to Guam and the Philippine Islands in the Pacific.

The Americans saw Corregidor as more than a way station en route to Manila. The island became a sentry in the mouth of the bay on which they built Fort Mills in 1908. American engineers constructed enormous seacoast batteries atop the island's cliffs, decked out with heavy coastal guns riveted into huge concrete pits. The engineers designed the gun mounts so that they could be mechanically raised and then lowered between shots, disappearing behind thick concrete walls to protect them from naval fire. Besides batteries and fortifications, the engineers paved sixty-five miles of roads and trails, and laid nineteen and a half miles of electric railroad track used to move equipment and ammunition to the different batteries that dotted the head of the island, dubbed Topside.

Built as a weapon of war, Fort Mills was reputed to be one of the finest forts in the Far East, both in military might and in amenities. For the American troops stationed there, it had an electric trolley system for public transport, a movie theater, a baseball field, a parade field, a swimming pool, and a nine-hole golf course.

But Fort Mills—built on an ancient hunk of volcanic rock in the mouth of the bay—had grown into much more than a fort. It was a symbol of America's might in the Pacific.

Until the Japanese arrived.

It was 1941 and the Japanese Imperial Army was on the march south with their sights set on Australia. Standing in their way was a ragtag force of American and Filipino soldiers under the command of Gen. Douglas MacArthur, the iconic general with his corncob pipe, neatly pressed uniform, and aviator sunglasses.

Even before World War II, MacArthur was an American legend: a hero of the Great War, a reformer of West Point, the youngest major general in US Army history, and a controversial army chief of staff. After retiring in 1935, MacArthur accepted an offer to become the Philippine Army's field marshal, tasked with training the country's fledgling military force in advance of independence in 1946. After Japan's surprise attack on Pearl Harbor and the subsequent invasion of the Philippines,

MacArthur was called back to the US Army to fight the Japanese. He set up his headquarters on Corregidor.

For three months, American and Filipino soldiers fought the Japanese on Luzon's Bataan Peninsula, which lay just over two miles across the sea from Corregidor's imposing cliffs. MacArthur's strategy relied on reinforcements and supplies from the United States to relieve his forces both on the peninsula and on Corregidor. But thanks to the enormous strain of fighting a war on two fronts—Washington had declared war against Germany three days after the announcement to fight Japan—it could take years for American reinforcements to arrive in the Philippines. There were no reinforcements and no supplies waiting in Australia either.

MacArthur—and the American and Filipino soldiers in his command—were on their own.

In February 1942, MacArthur wired President Franklin D. Roosevelt that he and his family would "share the fate of the garrison" on Corregidor, which looked like either surrender or death. But Roosevelt and the army's current chief of staff, Gen. George C. Marshall, had other plans.

At sixty-one, MacArthur was one of the most experienced generals in the United States, especially in the Pacific, and widely viewed as the only general who knew how to beat the Japanese. Losing his leadership would be as disastrous as the attack on Pearl Harbor. Plus, MacArthur was the overwhelming choice to command Allied Forces in the southwest Pacific. Knowing that America could not afford to lose the life of such a man, President Roosevelt ordered MacArthur to leave Corregidor.

He reluctantly followed the order in March 1942. From the deck of PT-41, a patrol boat sent to smuggle him out under the cover of darkness, MacArthur watched Corregidor's cliffs fade as he, his family, and a small contingent of staff officers headed for Australia. The flotilla of four PT boats fought stormy seas and dodged Japanese patrols for two days before getting to Mindanao, an island in the southern Philippines, where MacArthur's party boarded a flight to Australia.

Back on Bataan and Corregidor, the fighting continued. The Americans and Filipinos held out for two more months, even though victory seemed unlikely. Bataan fell first. American and Filipino soldiers surrendered on April 9, 1942.

The last escape from Corregidor came on May 3. The USS *Spearfish* slipped past the Japanese blockade and evacuated twenty-five people: staff officers and women from the hospital. The hospital's chief nurse refused to leave the wounded.

"I had enough faith in that old tunnel that I could make it if the Japs came in," she told Maj. Gen. Jonathan M. Wainwright, who took command of the defense after MacArthur's evacuation.

Thousands lived in Corregidor's Malinta Tunnel, which had been built by the Army Corps of Engineers under a hill in the middle of the island. It resembled a fish skeleton, the main tunnel acting as a backbone with twenty-four laterals branching like ribs. It started as a storage area, but during the siege, the tunnel became a refuge against Japanese shellfire. One lateral was turned into a thousand-bed hospital.

Two days after the *Spearfish* left, Japanese forces led by Maj.

Gen. Kureo Taniguchi struck the final blow. Using barges, almost eight hundred Japanese soldiers landed around four A.M. in the middle of the island after an intense artillery barrage.

There was no way of holding out any longer, especially with Japanese soldiers on the island. General Wainwright called a meeting with Gen. Lewis Beebe, his chief of staff, and Gen. George Moore, commander of the Harbor Defenses of Manila and Subic Bays, to discuss surrender.

"Maybe we could last through this day, but the end must certainly come tonight," Wainwright said. "It would be better to clear up the situation now, in daylight. What do you think?"

Beebe agreed with Wainwright.

"I think we should send a flag of truce through the lines right now," Beebe said.

Wainwright followed his advice.

"Tell the Nips we'll cease firing at noon," he said.

As Beebe and Moore left to broadcast the surrender message to the Japanese and to the American defenders, Wainwright sat down at his desk in the tunnel and wrote a note to President Roosevelt. "It is with broken heart and head bowed in sadness, but not in shame, that I report to Your Excellency that I must go today to arrange terms for the surrender of the fortified islands of Manila Bay," he wrote. "There is a limit to human endurance and that limit has long been past. Without prospect of relief I feel it is my duty to my country and to my gallant troops to end this useless effusion of blood and human sacrifice."

When the Japanese landed two tanks, enemy troops began moving off the beach toward Malinta Tunnel. This was the end.

The unthinkable had happened. The Japanese had been at war for years against the Chinese, and had surprised the American Navy at Pearl Harbor. Now they had taken this symbol of American might.

As Japanese soldiers closed on Malinta Tunnel, Irving Strobing, an army radioman, tapped out a final message in Morse code to his brother, Joe, and his family. That last message from Corregidor was sent at 11:05 A.M. and picked up by radio operators on the West Coast of the United States. "We've got about fifty-five minutes left and I feel sick at my stomach," Strobing broadcast.

I am really low down. They are around smashing rifles. They bring in the wounded every minute. We will be waiting for you guys to help. This is the only thing I guess that can be done. General Wainwright is a right guy, and we are willing to go on for him. But shells were dropping all night, faster than hell. Damage terrific. Too much for guys to take. Everyone is bawling like a baby. They are piling dead and wounded in our tunnel. The jig is up. Tell Joe, wherever he is, to give 'em hell for us. My love to you all. God bless you and keep you. Sign my name, and tell mother how you heard from me. Stand by.

Then, silence.

CHAPTER 1

Panama Jones and
His Three Thousand Thieves

FIRST LT. BILL Calhoun felt two rough hands shake him awake. The tropical sun was blinding as he opened his eyes and tried to focus on the massive shadow over him. Slowly, the grizzled, unshaven face of an Aussie bulldozer driver, wearing a broad smile, came into focus.

"Merry Christmas, Yank," the man said in his thick Australian accent.

"Merry Christmas," Calhoun muttered back, sitting up and rubbing his eyes.

The Aussie moved on, and after a moment, Calhoun climbed out of his bedroll and stood in the morning brightness, lighting his first cigarette of the day. He was a lean young man, only twenty-two, with a thin mustache and wavy, thick dark hair. Despite his youth, he had a western gunfighter's seasoned squint, and at times his mouth wore a mischievous smirk. Like millions of young American men, he was far from home, fighting a war

9

that sprawled from one end of the planet to the other. But unlike most, he wore the jump boots of a paratrooper.

All around him the forty paratroopers in his unit climbed out of bunkers and fighting positions to stretch stiff joints or light up their own smokes. Calhoun was their leader, in charge of F Company's first platoon. The Aussie who had awoken him was part of a construction crew tasked with building an airfield on Mindoro Island, which the men of the 503rd Parachute Infantry Regiment had taken only days before. Mindoro's expanse of flat sugarcane fields made it an ideal location from which to launch fighters, bombers, and transports in preparation for General MacArthur's upcoming assault on Manila, which lay less than two hundred miles north.

It was December 1944, and for the last two and a half years, American forces in the Pacific had been slowly island-hopping toward Tokyo. At first the war had gone well for Japan, with the seizure of the Philippines, as well as strategic islands that had been occupied by the Dutch and the British. But with a punishing defeat at the hands of the US Navy at Midway, Japan's crusade had begun to sour, and General MacArthur's victory in New Guinea had accelerated their crisis. Back in 1942, MacArthur had famously declared, in reference to the Philippines, "I shall return." And now, as America was grinding into a fourth year of global war, US troops were indeed closing in on Manila. MacArthur's plan was to begin the invasion of Luzon, where Manila was located, soon.

Calhoun and his paratroopers of the 503rd had arrived on Mindoro not from the belly of a C-47 but across the ramp of an

LCI, or Landing Craft, Infantry. They were met not by a well-armed and dug-in enemy force but by an uncontested beach. American patrols encountered only light resistance. After several days of stalking the island's jungles, Calhoun got a new mission: defend the nascent airfield and Australian construction crew against any Japanese harassment that might emerge from the brush.

Such an order was an insult for the paratroopers of the 503rd Parachute Infantry Regiment. It was bad enough that they had arrived in LCIs, like regular infantry. They didn't see themselves as guards. They were combat troops, the very same men who had made the first combat parachute assault in the Pacific theater.

They were the Airborne, for chrissakes.

Airborne units were still new to the army. The Soviets had been the first to test parachute assaults, but the German attack on Crete in 1941, during which some twenty thousand German paratroopers dropped onto the Allied-held fortress and seized it in a brutal two-week battle, was the catalyst. It was the first large airborne invasion at the time, and though the Germans had suffered heavy losses, the success of their Fallschirmjäger reminded American generals that the United States badly needed their own airborne troops to be combat-ready. The US Army was already testing the concept. Soldiers from the Twenty-Ninth Infantry Division formed a test platoon of airborne infantry. It conducted the first US Army parachute jump from a B-18 over Lawson Army Airfield at Fort Benning, Georgia, in August 1940.

Two years later, in November 1942, the 509th Parachute

Infantry Regiment jumped into North Africa during Operation Torch. While the Eighty-Second Airborne Division and later the 101st Airborne Division stood up to fight in Europe, it was the 503rd Parachute Infantry Regiment that was sent to Australia in 1942 to act as General MacArthur's strategic reserve. It was the only independent airborne regiment in the Pacific theater, adopting for its patch a wildcat parachuting from the sky baring its claws and its fangs.

Before departing for the Pacific, paratroopers from B Company were ordered to Salt Lake City, Utah, in January 1942 to train on skis. Soon photographs of paratroopers on skis appeared in newspapers, with a caption about how the men were learning "to fight efficiently on sledded feet," training they would never use in the Pacific. America's war was in its infancy, and the training was a ruse meant to convince Adolf Hitler that the Americans were planning to invade Norway. Not long after the training, the 503rd was sent to Panama on its way to Australia.

The 503rd made its first combat parachute jump in 1943. The assault on Nadzab, New Guinea, was an example of how an airborne operation was done, with one hitch: there were no Japanese in the area. The unit's second jump, on Noemfoor in July 1944, was a disaster because the C-47 cargo planes dropped the paratroopers from too low.

Calhoun joined the 503rd while the unit was in New Guinea, after the jump at Nadzab. He started as an assistant platoon leader before his platoon leader was transferred back to the rear base in Australia. He took command of F Company's first platoon and saw his first combat action during operations on Noemfoor, an island off the northern coast of New Guinea. The paratroopers were called in after the initial assault to help mop up Japanese resistance.

One day, Calhoun led his platoon into a jungle flanked by two ridges. After clearing the valley of Japanese, Calhoun and his platoon sergeant climbed to the top of one of the ridges to collect the third squad, which was dug in covering the rest of the platoon. The ridge was steep, with a crown of heavy brush, vines, and small trees. The brush was dense, making movement tricky. Calhoun fought through the undergrowth for a couple hundred feet, hacking a corridor for his platoon sergeant to follow. It was so thick, Calhoun figured there was little chance of there being any Japanese hiding nearby.

Then a shot rang out.

A jolt of pain shot up Calhoun's body. His right calf was on fire. The gunfire was so close, he felt the heat from the muzzle blast on his skin. He staggered back and his right leg collapsed. Calhoun fell to the ground.

Another shot rang out.

The bullet passed his face near his right eyebrow.

Calhoun rolled onto his stomach. The platoon sergeant heard the shot and moved back into the brush for cover.

"You OK?" Calhoun yelled back to his platoon sergeant.

"Yes," the sergeant said. "What happened?"

"Jap up ahead," Calhoun said. "I'm hit. I'm going back to the platoon. You go get third squad."

Calhoun crawled back through the hole in the brush. He made it back to the clearing, where his platoon waited. Second Lt. Emory Ball, his assistant platoon leader, met him halfway down the ridge with several other paratroopers. The medic cut away the back of Calhoun's pants near his buttocks.

"You're in the wrong place," Calhoun said. "It's my calf."

The medic ignored him. Calhoun said it again. Finally, the medic scolded him.

"Dammit, Lieutenant, I can see."

Nearby, paratroopers were building a litter. When Calhoun spotted it, he shook his head.

"You're not carrying me," he said. "I'm walking."

Calhoun stood up, took a step, and his right leg failed. He fell on his face. He didn't argue about the litter after that. The medic gave him morphine for the pain. As the platoon moved out, they heard firing. Another patrol spotted the Japanese soldier who had shot Calhoun coming down the ridge and killed him.

Col. George Jones's own launch evacuated Calhoun to a nearby hospital. On the boat, Jones, the normally taciturn commander of the 503rd, quipped, "You must have wanted a Purple Heart pretty bad to give up a piece of ass to get it."

At the hospital, doctors told Calhoun the bullet had entered his right buttock near the hip joint, grazed his sciatic nerve, and exited an inch from his spine. While he recovered, Calhoun found out that he had indeed earned a Purple Heart. The award was given to all soldiers wounded in combat. But Calhoun saw the award as validation—he was a combat veteran now.

ON MINDORO, THE soldiers of the 503rd endured their guard duty, waiting for their next combat mission. The only excitement came when General MacArthur gifted the outfit a shipment of frozen turkeys. Calhoun's platoon gleefully built roaring fires and roasted the big birds on spits, turning them for hours. Just after noon, a large spread was set and the paratroopers moved down the line, filling their plates with meat. Calhoun savored each bite because it reminded him of home.

The paratroopers were free the rest of the day.

F Company had never been into nearby San Jose, and Calhoun followed the others into town. It was made up of frame houses, built near a three-story sugar refinery with a tower. The paratroopers congregated near the center of town and gave out pieces of hard candy to kids. Calhoun watched as each child received one piece. Most got back in line. No one stopped them—they'd suffered enough under Japanese occupation. The candy was a small reward for years of inhumane treatment.

After the New Year, with the threat of a Japanese counterattack on Mindoro over, the 503rd moved out of their defensive positions. They set up a camp with pyramidal tents in the sun-drenched valley of the Bugsanga River bottom. About three thousand men lived at the camp while Australian construction crews finished the airfields.

The 503rd had a reputation for "liberating" equipment and supplies from other units. The paratroopers noticed other units had refrigeration trucks and base headquarters had beer stacked up on pallets nearby. The paratroopers wanted the same.

When a general commands a division, he sees that his troops get supplies like fresh food, new equipment, and uniforms. The 503rd had no general. Their thirty-one-year-old commander, George Jones, was only a colonel. A member of the 1935 class of West Point, Jones used to joke that he had graduated in the 93rd percentile—if you looked at the rankings from the bottom up. He had been commissioned in the infantry, and after serving in various units he volunteered for the Airborne soon after parachute school at Fort Benning. He was the thirty-first officer to qualify as a paratrooper.

After earning his wings, the badge awarded to all soldiers who complete jump training, Jones was stationed in the Panama Canal Zone, first as a company commander and then taking full command of the 501st Parachute Battalion, one of the army's first airborne units. That assignment had earned him the nickname "Panama Jones." He was also called "the Warden" after he caught several junior officers sneaking beer on the ship from Panama to Australia and confined them to their staterooms.

After the United States declared war, the 501st was absorbed by the 503rd on its way to Australia. As a lieutenant colonel, Jones served as the regimental executive officer until after the Nadzab mission in 1943, when the first commander, Col. Kenneth Kinsler, committed suicide. Jones was bumped up to full-bird colonel and assumed command before the landings on Mindoro. A professional soldier, he drew a distinction between the citizen soldiers who made up most of his ranks and the career officers.

Since Jones wasn't a general, the 503rd was low on the priority list when it came to supplies and amenities. Jones may have lacked the clout of a general, but he was persistent enough to get the cigarettes he wanted. He preferred Chesterfields, but when he got ration packs with lesser brands, he asked his subordinate officers to trade him their Chesterfields. As he outranked them, the officers wouldn't refuse.

With no aboveboard means of getting what they needed and wanted, the paratroopers became experts in requisitioning. That's the reason the unit was nicknamed "Panama Jones and His Three Thousand Thieves." They'd looted the surrounding bases in New Guinea, and on Mindoro, as soon as the threat of Japanese attacks passed, they started in on their neighboring camps. It wasn't uncommon for a soldier to lose a jeep when men from the 503rd were around. Once the paratroopers acquired a vehicle, a new serial number found its way onto the left-side frame rail behind the front bumper on the driver's side, and the jeep was theirs. Few mastered the art of procurement better than Calhoun's good friend First Lt. Edward Flash.

Flash, formerly a platoon sergeant in the 503rd's G Company, had graduated from the US Army Officer Candidate School in Brisbane and was assigned as the second-platoon leader in F Company. In New Guinea, he displayed his new leadership chops by pulling off some great capers. When the 503rd camp was issued a 220-volt generator, Flash needed 220-volt bulbs to light their tents. The bulbs were stored in a canvas tent surrounded by a wood fence and protected by a watchful Australian supply sergeant, who refused to give them over without the proper requisition papers. Flash knew he couldn't get the right signatures, at least without headaches. Instead, he grabbed Calhoun and asked him to go in and talk with the supply sergeant. Make nice, keep him distracted, Flash told him.

Calhoun went in and stopped at the supply sergeant's desk. He knew his mission, and asked for "blue goose" ammo—incendiary bullets—for F Company's machine guns. The Australians had planes with .30-caliber machine guns, which was the same caliber as the paratroopers' light machine guns, but Calhoun was pretty sure the sergeant didn't have the ammunition, which was likely stored in a different supply tent.

"You have to requisition the ordnance supply at Dobodura," the supply sergeant told Calhoun, who smiled and played dumb.

"How do you get there?"

While the sergeant gave Calhoun directions, Flash walked past, avoiding eye contact with the sergeant at the desk, and disappeared into the rows of supplies. The sergeant hadn't noticed him enter. Moments later, Flash came out carrying a box of bulbs. The sergeant looked up as Flash passed by.

"Stop!" the sergeant barked. "Hey, you there! Stop!"

Flash ignored him and walked to his jeep parked outside. He put the box in the back and drove off without a backward glance. The sergeant looked at Calhoun, who just shrugged.

"Thanks for the directions," he said, and walked out of the tent.

Calhoun strode down the road until he was out of sight of the supply tent. He found Flash waiting with the jeep and a smirk.

Mission accomplished.

By the time the paratroopers left New Guinea, their camp was comfortable and well stocked. On Mindoro, the 503rd were back to square one. Provided with just the essentials—tents and cots—the paratroopers set out to improve their living conditions. One of the first tasks was to procure storage racks to keep gear off the ground and to dry it after long patrols in the nearby jungles. When Flash spotted a pile of lumber earmarked to make flooring for tents at a military police battalion's camp, the paratroopers backed a stolen truck up to the lumber pile and loaded it up.

With no mission to prepare for, the paratroopers were forced to live in garrison. That meant seemingly endless hours of guard duty, with nothing to look forward to besides meals and an occasional movie. When there wasn't work to be done, the nearby town offered paratroopers things that camp couldn't—namely, girls. As long as a paratrooper was present at roll call at the end of the day and the following morning, no one much cared where he went at night. It wasn't long before a worn path appeared between the camp and the town.

As the days passed, the 503rd's only enemy was boredom. So, when a sergeant came looking for truck drivers, Pfc. Anthony Lopez, a short Hispanic kid from Colorado with thick black hair, jumped at the chance to finally do something.

He'd learned how to drive trucks before he joined the army. The youngest of five brothers, Lopez had grown up without a father, but in the army he found a new family. He graduated from high school in April 1943 and enlisted in the military. He did it in part because it was expected. It was World War II and young men were expected to serve.

But most of all, the army was a steady job.

Soldiering agreed with him. He liked the marching and working out, and learned on the range he was a deadly shot, earning 195 points out of a possible 200 on his marksmanship test. The score was a training-battalion record at the time.

When an Airborne recruiter came to his camp during basic training offering fifty dollars extra for jump pay, Lopez signed up. He went to airborne school at Fort Benning and was assigned to F Company, 503rd Parachute Infantry Regiment. He joined the unit in Brisbane, Australia, in July 1944 and made the combat jump on Noemfoor Island soon after. By the time he was stuck in the monotony of garrison duty on Mindoro, he was an assistant squad leader in F Company's second platoon.

The sergeant took Lopez down to the docks and got him behind the wheel of a deuce-and-a-half truck. Putting it into gear, Lopez backed it down to the jetty, where landing craft were ferrying in supplies.

The loaders didn't ask Lopez any questions. They filled his truck with the next load and handed him the manifest with the destinations. Lopez followed the dirt roads that crisscrossed the river bottom and dropped the supplies at the different tent cities that housed the myriad American units island-hopping north toward Japan. For two weeks, Lopez delivered supplies. One afternoon when he was off duty down by the beach, his friend George Pierce pulled him aside.

"Why don't we grab a truck?" Pierce said. "We'll just back in there. They don't ask you nothing. They just load your truck, give you the manifest, and you're on your way."

"Where can we get a truck?" Lopez said.

"Well, there's a bunch of Aussies over here," Pierce said, pointing to a camp near the jetty. "They've got trucks."

They walked over to the Australian camp and found some soldiers in the motor pool.

"You guys have a truck we can borrow?" Pierce asked. "We've got to take a load of stuff to the company."

"Sure, mate," one of the Australian soldiers said. "Take it. Take it. Just bring it back."

Lopez and Pierce climbed in, and they drove the truck down to the jetty. Lopez backed it up to the loading area and in a few minutes, it was full of supplies. A sergeant handed Pierce the manifest and he signed it with an *X* on the signature line. Lopez put the truck in gear and it rumbled down the dirt road to the 503rd's area.

The paratroopers cheered when Lopez pulled the truck into F Company's camp. They swarmed the back, pulling out boxes of coffee, square cans of chicken, apples, flour, sugar, and milk. The company took half of the supplies, and Lopez donated the other half to the Australians when he returned the truck.

Back at camp, Lopez was met with confused faces. The paratroopers inventoried their loot, but they weren't sure what to do with some of it. Rummaging through a pile of cans and boxes, he found flour and canned apples, and thought of his mother.

"Hey, do you guys want to have some apple pie?" Lopez said.

"Where are we going to get pie?" one paratrooper said.

"Well, we've got canned apples there," Lopez said, pointing to the ingredients. "We've got those great big pans. We can cut them square and have a square baking pan."

Pierce laughed and said, "You know how to make pies?"

"Yeah, I do," Lopez said.

He had learned how to cook by watching his mother. She worked as a seamstress in a jeans factory during the day and as a cook at a Mexican restaurant at night to make ends meet. He'd join her in the kitchen to help, and picked up a few skills.

Lopez's platoon mates were skeptical, but followed his directions. F Company was camped in a dried canal bed with five-foot-tall sidewalls. The paratroopers dug out an "oven" in one of the sides. While Lopez mixed lard, flour, and baking powder, the other paratroopers gathered wood and heated the oven.

Lopez laid the crust into the square pans and then filled it with canned apples and sugar. He covered the top with dough and a layer of sugar. He had enough ingredients for a couple of pies.

As the pies baked in the dugout oven, Flash, Lopez's platoon leader, and First Lt. Bill Bailey, F Company's commander, smelled the familiar aroma as they walked by. Lopez and the others waved the officers over.

"Hey, you guys, you want some pie?"

"Oh sure, yeah," Flash said, taking a cup of coffee and a slice of pie. "You bet."

For a few bites, the war came second to the most American of pies. When the last one was baked, Lopez was treated like a hero. The pies were a hit. He did such a good job his friends begged him to join the mess hall as a cook.

Lopez refused.

"No," he said. "I'm no cook."

With the exception of Lopez's apple pie, the food in camp was dull. Army cooks prepared everything from a can, with little seasoning. The only redeeming quality was that it was hot. Sick and tired of the bland chow, Pvt. Chet Nycum, G Company's lead scout, organized a hunting party looking for fresh meat.

It was a job that suited him, for Nycum was a man at home in the wilderness. When the Japanese attacked Pearl Harbor back in 1941, Nycum, already serving in the army, was on leave, hunting deer in Pennsylvania. He was working as an X-ray technician at the Fort Meade hospital in Maryland when one day a friend showed him a notice from the bulletin board calling for volunteers to join the parachute troops. Both Nycum and his friend requested a transfer, but Nycum was married and the parachute regiment didn't take married men without a waiver from their wife. Nycum's wife, Margaret, reluctantly signed, and his transfer was approved.

He went to Fort Benning for basic training with the 501st Parachute Battalion. After completing the required five jumps, Nycum got his wings and headed to Fort Bragg, North Carolina, for advanced training. He was part of the first full regiment of paratroopers in the US Army before being transferred to the 503rd. After joining the unit, he fought in New Guinea, making a combat jump at Noemfoor before landing in Mindoro.

As a scout, Nycum typically carried a Thompson submachine gun, so before leaving for the hunt he borrowed a semiautomatic M1 Garand, which was better suited for taking down an animal. Or so he assumed. He took his Thompson submachine gun along just in case. The hunting party liberated a truck and went out looking for carabao, a water buffalo native to the Philippines.

After scouring the grasslands that made up most of the island, the paratroopers camped near a river. Using grenades, they killed a mess of fresh fish for dinner. The explosions attracted an elderly Filipino man who lived nearby. He asked the paratroopers for their discarded fish heads, which he cooked up with his rice. Nycum and the others asked the man if he'd seen any carabao. He pointed over a hill and explained in broken English and hand gestures that a bull took over his herd and attacked him whenever he came near. The next day, the elderly Filipino returned to the camp and led the paratroopers to the bull.

Carabao are massive animals with thick, curved horns and round, stout bodies. An apron of flesh hung from the bull's neck. The paratroopers pulled the truck parallel to the river and walked over to the bull, which was in the water staring at the approaching men.

"Let him have the first shot," one of the paratroopers said, and handed the elderly Filipino an M1 Garand.

The man shouldered the rifle and fired. The bullet hit the bull in the apron, but the beast didn't go down. The bullet just pissed it off. The bull raised its head and zeroed in on the group of men. It snorted and stomped and pawed its hooves. The paratroopers and the elderly Filipino backed away until their backs were against the truck.

Then the bull charged.

The paratroopers opened fire. Nycum watched his eight-round clip eject from the M1 and turned back to the truck. All around him the paratroopers kept firing as the bull closed on them. Nycum snatched his Thompson submachine gun and chambered a round.

The bull was at point-blank range as Nycum pulled the trigger. The Thompson unleashed a stream of bullets. Nycum kept the trigger squeezed until he heard only a click. Just as the magazine was spent, the bull fell. Another two feet, and it would have gored him.

Lowering the smoking submachine gun, Nycum noticed the hide from the bull's skull was missing from where the .45-caliber bullets had bounced off the bone. Nycum dubbed it the "banzai bull," after the frontal charges used by Japanese troops. One of the paratroopers volunteered to remove the guts. Driving his trench knife into the underbelly, he cut the length of the bull's belly, spilling the intestines and other organs onto the grass.

The smell was unbearable.

Nycum and the others covered their faces with kerchiefs. Nycum laughed when he saw everyone. The paratroopers looked like bandits in a western movie. After the bull was dressed, the paratroopers took the hindquarters and loaded them into the truck. The rest was left with the elderly Filipino.

Back at camp, the great hunters delivered the meat to the cooks for dinner. After cleaning up, Nycum and the others arrived at the mess tent with their mouths watering. Getting a slab of meat, they sat at the table ready to devour their prize when all around him Nycum heard grumbling.

One bite and Nycum understood.

The meat was tough.

Nycum chewed his piece and sucked out the juices before discarding the pulp. There wasn't a set of human teeth that could cut through it, he thought. But even though dinner was a failure, the hunt had broken up the boredom of garrison life. The next time Nycum would fire his weapon, he'd be doing it in combat.

CHAPTER 2

Field Order Number 9

COLONEL JONES PEERED through the Plexiglas nose of a B-25 bomber.

Strapped into the machine gunner's seat, he could see the island of Corregidor coming into view. From the air, it looked like a massive tadpole swimming out to sea. All around him the aircrew prepared to attack targets on the Bataan Peninsula, but Jones was focused on the "head" of the tadpole, dubbed Topside, as it slipped underneath the bomber's wings. The pilot made a couple of low runs over the island as Jones searched for suitable landing fields for his paratroopers.

The day before, a courier from Gen. Walter Krueger's headquarters had arrived at the 503rd's camp on Mindoro with a sealed pouch. Inside, Jones found a written order naming him the commander of "Rock Force," consisting of the 503rd and the Third Battalion of the Thirty-Fourth Infantry Regiment from the Twenty-Fourth Infantry Division. The force was tapped to retake Corregidor.

After receiving the order, Jones left Mindoro for the Sixth Army headquarters in Gerona, a small town on the highway and railroad line north of Manila. He arrived on an olive-drab single-engine army observation plane and found the headquarters in a makeshift building in town. Lt. Col. Jack Tolson, his former regimental executive officer now working operations for the Sixth Army, met him at the headquarters.

The upcoming invasion of Japan would require Manila to be the main logistical base. Anything shipped to Manila would pass the guns on Corregidor and negotiate the minefields, which were the underwater gates to the entrances to the most valuable port in the archipelago. Prior to the war, the US Navy had installed mines in the harbor, which were detonated by control panels on Corregidor. Planners wanted to regain control of the panels and disarm the mines. Until the mines were cleared, entering the harbor was unsafe.

But deep down, Corregidor represented American strength in the Pacific. Retaking the island would erase the memory of Wainwright's surrender in 1942. To Douglas MacArthur, it was even more personal. After his escape from the island, he had been awarded the Medal of Honor for his defense of the Philippines—a defense, of course, that had resulted in surrender. American officials knew that the American people, shocked by the attacks on Pearl Harbor, needed someone to rally behind. Giving MacArthur the medal was in part to make him a hero in the eyes of a shaken citizenry.

But public support masked a deep resentment by rank-and-file soldiers left behind on Bataan and Corregidor. They pegged MacArthur with the derisive nickname "Dugout Doug," claiming he hid safely in Malinta Tunnel while they had endured Japanese bombing and shelling. In their minds, he left behind 78,000 American troops with no hope of reinforcements, and for his efforts he was awarded the nation's highest medal for valor.

Taking back the Philippines—an island chain MacArthur had called home for years—would be the crowning achievement of his campaign to drive the Japanese out of the archipelago. And taking back Corregidor would prove his valor.

The Sixth Army had concluded that a parachute assault was the only way to get troops safely onto the island. Planners were not eager to repeat the bloody amphibious landings at Tarawa, which had cost the Marine Corps almost four thousand killed or wounded. But Tolson admitted there were few landing fields suitable for the assault. Tolson gave Jones the latest maps and aerial photos of Corregidor. Jones arranged a ride with a bomber crew so he could do a reconnaissance of the island and select landing fields.

From the nose of the bomber, the condition of the island made Jones just as nervous as the small landing zones. Topside was in ruins. The concrete buildings that once stood pristine— making Fort Mills a choice posting—had been shattered by Japanese and American bombs. The prewar barracks and officer houses had crumbling walls and mangled roofs. Craters and blasted rock made the island a moonscape, and particularly treacherous for paratroopers because each pile of debris or broken tree could injure or kill a descending soldier before he had a chance to fire a shot in anger.

On one of the passes, Jones spotted two clearings on Topside. One was the old nine-hole golf course. The other was the parade field. Jones made note of both on his map. Another possible landing spot was Kindley Field, an old airstrip at the narrow tail of the island. The airstrip was overgrown and out of use, but it was flat and free of the ankle-breaking debris on Topside. Jones circled Kindley Field. After the reconnaissance flight, he radioed the Sixth Army's headquarters his selection.

But General Krueger vetoed it, instead selecting the parade ground and golf course. Krueger, a World War I veteran who had risen from private to general, was known as a skillful tactician, aggressive when he attacked and tenacious on the defense. "A drop there would have exposed the paratroopers to devastating fire from Malinta Hill [which sat between Topside and Kindley Field] and Topside," Krueger wrote later. "It seemed better to me to make the drop on Topside itself, where the Japanese were not likely to expect it to be made."

Krueger was right.

The Imperial High Command wasn't prepared for a parachute assault. RAdm. Sanji Iwabuchi assigned his executive officer, Capt. Akira Itagaki, to defend Corregidor with four thousand naval and army troops as well as a Shinyo suicide boat squadron. Japanese planners warned Itagaki of an airborne attack, but being a sailor, he dismissed the idea because of Corregidor's rough terrain. He was sure the Americans would strike from the sea, and the Japanese defenses were set up against an amphibious attack.

With the decision made, Jones and his staff started working on the details. The landing fields were small compared to the ones in France during D-Day or in Holland during Market Garden. The parade ground was 325 yards long and 250 yards wide, while the golf course was slightly larger at 350 yards long but narrower at 185 yards wide. Both landing fields stood out as relatively clear areas surrounded by a border of tangled trees and underbrush that fell off into steep cliffs or ravines. Miss the landing field and a paratrooper was likely headed into a jungle ravine or out to sea.

But the paratroopers had no choice if they wanted to execute the plan.

Jones huddled with his staff and senior commanders in the command tent on Mindoro. Planners built a massive sand table with a replica of the island, and Jones and his staff started to brief the 503rd's senior commanders.

WHILE COLONEL JONES planned, the paratroopers waited, bored and restless. They'd already been alerted several times since Christmas—at least once to jump on Nichols Field near Manila— only to have the mission canceled. The 503rd paratroopers were forced to watch the Eleventh Airborne Division—a junior unit, since it was stood up after the 503rd—fly overhead on their way to Luzon to help liberate Manila. In the 503rd's mind, it was their mission and they were being left out of the fight. What the paratroopers didn't know was that Jones had talked to the

Eleventh Airborne Division about attaching the 503rd to the mission, but was instead told that MacArthur intended to send the 503rd to retake Corregidor.

A cloud hung over the camp after the Eleventh Airborne jump. Morale was low because the rank and file had no idea what was in the works. Things changed once the plan was briefed to the battalion commanders and senior staff. The rumor mill was churning with talk of a new mission. But none of the paratroopers bought in until they got it official.

On the morning of February 12, 1945, Jones and his staff finally released Field Order Number 9, the plan to retake Corregidor. Jones, standing in front of the sand table, walked his commanders through the plan. Maj. Lawson Caskey, the Second Battalion commander, was on his way back to brief the Second Battalion staff when he saw Capt. Charlie Bradford standing in front of his olive-green tent. Bradford was toweling off, having just returned from his morning swim.

Bradford noticed a spring in Caskey's step as he walked through camp.

"Hello, Doc," Caskey said. "Come over here. I've got some good news to tell you."

Bradford joined Caskey just out of earshot of the other tents. Bradford was Second Battalion's surgeon. A 1926 graduate of Harvard College, he was part of a team of Boston-area surgeons who traveled with the American Hospital Expedition to London during the Blitz to provide medical care in 1940. Two years later, he joined the army as a captain in the Medical Corps. An orthopedic surgeon, he had started his army career at a hospital near

Cairns. After setting several broken bones after a 503rd practice jump near Gordonvale, Bradford thought he'd be more useful in the regiment. He finagled jump training in North Queensland and qualified as a paratrooper.

"If you had your choice of the best combat jump our regiment could make, what objective would you pick?" Caskey said.

Bradford thought for a second. "Tokyo."

Caskey, a former private who'd worked his way into command of a battalion, laughed.

"No, seriously," he said. "Here in the Philippines."

"Manila, I suppose."

Caskey shook his head. The Philippine capital was burning and the Eleventh Airborne Division were already there.

"Well, there aren't any others that I know of," Bradford said. "What is it?"

Caskey smiled.

"Corregidor," he said.

Bradford was skeptical. He knew the island was small, only a little more than a mile wide at the head. The only drop zones were on the tail, where a small airfield was located. Caskey shook his head. The paratroopers were going to jump on Topside's parade field and golf course.

"That's the beauty of it," Caskey said. "The Japs will never expect it, because it looks impossible. No army in this war has pulled off anything like it. But our intelligence has got it all figured out, and they say it'll be as easy as opening a kit bag."

Every soldier knew that when intelligence says a mission is easy, it rarely is.

"How many Japs will be waiting for us?" Bradford said.

"We don't have any idea of the Jap strength," Caskey said. "Some say that the island has been taken over for a last stand by the Imperial Marines. If that's so, there could be eight or nine thousand of them. Others claim that they are keeping only a token force there. We'll see."

"Instead of dropping us on this rock pile," Bradford said, "why not send us in amphibious craft?"

That was the Japanese battle plan back in 1942 and it cost them, Caskey said. The beaches are well protected by machine guns and artillery. The key to the operation was holding the high ground.

"Our Marines lost a thousand killed in their beach landing at Tarawa, and three thousand five hundred killed or missing at Saipan, and neither of those posts had half the fortifications Corregidor has got," Caskey said. "When Wainwright held out against the Japs, he was subjected for a month to the heaviest kind of artillery barrages; but even after that, his men were still able to kill eight thousand Japs when they made their final amphibious assault. If we get down on Corregidor's Topside, we'll hold the center of the Jap position. Their unity will be destroyed. They may be all around us, but they'll have to climb up to get at us, and all the while, we'll be sitting pretty, waiting for 'em."

It sounded easy when Caskey laid it out, but Bradford knew it never was. Yet every paratrooper wanted the chance to jump on Corregidor. It was a worthy consolation prize if the Eleventh Airborne Division had gotten Manila.

Bill Calhoun heard the rumors about the jump on Corregidor, but didn't believe them until Caskey confirmed it when the regiment went on alert. All Second Battalion jumpmasters were called to the airfield for a practice jump. Once airborne, the jumpmasters were told to look for a fifty-foot circle of white tape. They could see it staked down in the grass from the air. With such small landing fields, it would be up to the jumpmasters to make sure each stick—or small group of paratroopers—hit the target.

After the men climbed into the C-47s, the planes sped down the runway and lifted off into blue skies. As they made passes over the target, Calhoun and the other jumpmasters tried to land in the circle. Calhoun hit it on his first try without difficulty.

The attack was planned in three phases. Fifty-one C-47s from the 317th Troop Carrier Group would arrive over the island at 8:30 A.M. on February 16. Calhoun's platoon and the rest of Second Battalion would follow at noon. First Battalion would jump the following morning.

Colonel Jones and the Third Battalion would lead the way. A company of engineers and a battery from the 462nd Parachute Field Artillery Battalion with four 75mm pack howitzers would jump with the first wave. They'd provide cover for the amphibious landing by the Thirty-Fourth Infantry. Caskey's Second Battalion would spearhead the second lift. Once on the ground, the second wave would join the first and push out to secure Topside and root out Japanese defenders. The last wave made up of First Battalion paratroopers would reinforce the whole regiment the next day.

By the first day, the paratroopers would consolidate on Topside and the Thirty-Fourth Infantry would take Malinta Hill. The second day, American forces would attempt to link up before rooting out the Japanese defenders hiding in the island's tunnel complex.

With the landing fields selected, the planners looked at weather and wind. The prevailing winds over Manila Bay blew from east to west. Using two columns of C-47s, the paratroopers would approach the island from the southwest at four hundred feet. The planes would be over the landing fields for six seconds per pass, meaning they'd have to jump in sticks of six to eight men. There would be only two aircraft over the landing fields at a time.

After the first pass, the planes would circle, one column to the right and the other column to the left, and make another pass. It would take three passes per plane to get everyone on Topside.

Despite the careful planning, Jones figured he'd lose between 20 and 50 percent of his men to injuries from the jump. But it was worth the risk to seize the high ground and force the Japanese to fight uphill to repel the invasion. On paper, the plan was risky but sound. But as the saying goes, no plan survives first contact.

The enemy always gets a vote.

Back on Mindoro, mission briefings for the companies began two days before the jump. A "war" tent was set up on an open plain with its sides lashed down and sealed for operational security. The paratroopers didn't want the target to leak. A sand table with a model of the island sat in the middle of the tent. Calhoun and the rest of the platoon leaders got maps of the island. Except for Malinta Hill and Topside, the maps lacked the names of the ridges, hills, and ravines. None of the buildings were named nor had labels with their purposes. Roads and trail names were a mystery. The maps didn't show the tunnel systems that ran underneath the hills either.

Instead, numbers marked the different batteries and road intersections on the south end of the island. On the north end, letters were used. When the paratroopers asked for updated maps with the tunnels, they were told the tunnel systems were classified. Once on the ground, the paratroopers created their own naming system, or when they spotted a sign they would update the map.

When it was first platoon, F Company's turn, Calhoun led his men into the war tent. He had thirty minutes to brief his platoon. He'd studied the plan with his company commander, First Lt. Bill Bailey, already. Now he needed to make sure his platoon of forty men knew what to do. They crowded into the tent. The flaps were closed and the sun heated up the cramped space like an oven.

With his paratroopers huddled around the table, all eyes on the map, Calhoun pointed out the parade field where they would land, and then drew a finger down to the company rally point. Designated 28-D, it was a house that sat at the western end of a row of senior officer homes, overlooking Crockett Ravine on the south side of the island. Once on the ground, they would be pushed out based on how the Japanese defenders reacted. By the time the briefing was over, the men's uniforms were soaked through with sweat. But morale was high. They had a mission. A purpose, even if it was fighting a fanatical enemy that wouldn't give an inch.

FOUGHT IN CLAUSTROPHOBIC jungles, often in close quarters, the war in the Pacific was particularly nasty. The American soldiers, sailors, and Marines hated the Japanese more than their foes in Europe. It came down to a simple fact: The Japanese had attacked the United States.

They started the war.

The Sixth Army estimated 850 Japanese defenders were on Corregidor. But reports from guerrillas about ships dropping troops and supplies off on the island suggested even more.

The Japanese were a tenacious enemy. They would often fight until the last man, especially if an officer was present, making them a formidable opponent. It was illegal to surrender in the Japanese military, or to permit oneself to be captured. To be captured meant that the soldier's name would be stricken from his family register kept at city hall. This would bring shame and dishonor to the family that would affect their future work and promotions. It was better to commit suicide than risk being wounded, or knocked out, and captured.

"Death is lighter than goose-down feathers; duty is heavier than a mountain range," was an oft-repeated Japanese saying.

Disobedience, or even discussion, was never an option. Disobeying a direct order from a superior meant at least a court-martial, and orders from officers were considered to be from the emperor himself. Disobeying a direct order from an officer could result in execution.

While the paratroopers prepared for battle, B-24 bombers from the 307th Bomb Group and A-20s from the 3rd Attack Group hammered the Japanese defenders near the end of January and continued right up to the 503rd's operation. The bombers dropped more than three thousand tons of explosives on the island, making it the heaviest concentration dropped in the Pacific war. When bombs weren't landing on Topside, navy ships in the mouth of Manila Bay bombarded the island's defenses.

The raids damaged the north and south docks. Each bombing run shattered the landscape, stripping parts of it bare of its naturally lush vegetation and leaving it scarred with craters and debris. Some of the regiment's planners rode in the bombers as they attacked the island. A lieutenant new to the Pacific theater took one of the final recon flights in a B-24. There was no antiaircraft fire, and the lieutenant didn't see a single man on the island. After he got back to Mindoro, he ran into Bradford. He told the doctor the Japanese were hardly garrisoning Corregidor.

After the lieutenant left, Bradford shook his head. The lieutenant was new and the doctor didn't trust his judgment. All Bradford knew for sure was they really had no idea how many Japanese they faced.

CHAPTER 3

To the Colors

THE DAY BEFORE the jump, the stockade was emptied. Most of the paratroopers being held for various charges were shuttled off to help with the loading and unloading of transports. They'd do the work others didn't want to do.

But not Pvt. Lloyd G. McCarter.

First Lt. Calhoun went down himself to get McCarter, a former squad leader and scout in first platoon. Calhoun had handpicked him to be the platoon's eyes and ears in New Guinea almost a year before, and despite the private's current stay behind bars, Calhoun was not going into combat without him.

The two best riflemen in each squad were usually chosen as scouts, but Calhoun's scouts rotated home soon after he took command of his platoon in New Guinea. He went searching for new candidates from a group of replacements who arrived in May 1944. Calhoun was looking through the replacement paratroopers' records when he stumbled upon McCarter's file.

McCarter was considered an old man in the platoon at the age of twenty-four. He was two years older than Calhoun. But his practical experience stood out. He had worked as a lumberjack in Idaho and Washington before joining the military. Calhoun needed someone familiar with working outdoors, but who was also dedicated to the job. It wasn't easy being the guy in front. Not only was he facing down any potential ambush, but he also had the platoon's life in his hands. Miss a sniper or booby trap, and one of his buddies could be wounded or, worse, killed. What stood out to Calhoun was McCarter's sacrifices in order to join the paratroopers. McCarter had started in the artillery but gave up his sergeant stripes when he volunteered for airborne school.

Calhoun found McCarter in a tent with the other replacements. He was short—only about five feet six inches tall—but had a barrel chest and thick, muscular forearms. Calhoun pulled him aside and pitched him the scout job. McCarter was skeptical.

"I don't have any infantry training, sir," McCarter said.

That didn't bother Calhoun. He knew he could teach him tactics, and besides, with no experience McCarter hadn't developed any bad habits to overcome. But first he needed to know that McCarter could handle a different kind of weapon from what he'd fired in basic training. Scouts carried the Thompson submachine gun, a weapon unfamiliar to McCarter. Invented by John T. Thompson in 1918, the submachine gun was the weapon of choice for gangsters during the Prohibition era. During World War II, it was also popular with paratroopers, rangers, and commandos because of its large .45-caliber cartridge and fully automatic fire.

"I've never fired a Thompson," McCarter told Calhoun when he asked about the submachine gun.

Calhoun called over one of the platoon's sergeants and told him to get a Thompson and take McCarter into the jungle with several magazines to show him how to operate the weapon. Paratroopers were trained to fire it from the hip, but after missing the target with the first magazine, McCarter turned the submachine gun on its side with the buttstock lying flat on his muscular forearm. The platoon sergeant watched as he fired several deadly accurate bursts into the target. It was unorthodox, but it worked for him and he was lethal. An hour later, the sergeant came back to Calhoun's tent with a smile. McCarter, he reported, was a natural.

Calhoun sent McCarter up to regiment. The 503rd was about to start jungle training, and regiment mustered all the scouts to run through a final test before the training course. The test was designed to check the scout's ability to pick out enemy positions along a jungle trail. Once spotted, the scouts opened fire on steel targets set up nearby. As McCarter and his partner entered the course, General Krueger, the Sixth Army commander who would later order the 503rd to attack Corregidor, arrived with Colonel Jones. The general was on an inspection tour and wanted to follow McCarter on the test course.

McCarter moved out, skipping on the balls of his feet in a peculiar, easy lope. The first target, a machine-gun emplacement, was in the V of two streams. The stream banks were fifteen feet high. The gunner was sitting beside the machine gun with his feet in a foxhole waiting for the scouts to come up the path.

McCarter spotted the gunner first and, arriving faster than expected, opened fire, hitting the target silhouette near the gun.

One of the slugs from the Thompson submachine gun just missed the gunner and struck the bolt handle on the machine gun. The startled gunner scrambled into the foxhole unharmed, but shaken. The exercise was paused and the instructors ordered the rest of the gunners into their foxholes. Only then was Mc-Carter allowed to continue his easy lope, mowing down the targets one after another. When it was over, Krueger left impressed and Calhoun had his lead scout.

Calhoun's confidence in McCarter soon paid off. The private was a natural. He demonstrated over and over again that if he couldn't see the enemy, he heard them, and if he didn't hear them, he smelled them. The guy had a bloodhound's nose. When the paratroopers ran into Japanese soldiers on other patrols, Mc-Carter often laughed and shouted insults as he attacked.

In the jungle of Noemfoor in July 1944, McCarter was leading a platoon down a trail surrounded by thick brush when a Japanese voice called out, challenging them. The platoon stopped in their tracks. McCarter, scanning the tangled jungle ahead, answered the Japanese call in a sharp "*Ho*." The Japanese soldier challenged McCarter again. McCarter cocked his head and zeroed in on the sound. He skipped forward on the trail's coral outcroppings like a ballet dancer as he charged ahead. Calhoun and the rest of the platoon picked up the pace just to keep up as McCarter heard another challenge from the Japanese sentry. He called back with the same sharp "*Ho*." The Japanese answered with a burst from a machine gun. The rounds shot down the trail. McCarter opened fire with his Thompson and charged forward on the balls of his feet.

Calhoun was third in line. He heard the staccato bursts of gunfire as McCarter advanced. When Calhoun got to the front of the platoon, he found four dead Japanese soldiers with a Nambu light machine gun in a fighting hole overlooking the trail. Even with the threat now neutralized, McCarter was still ramped up and excited. The fighting energized him. He seemed more alive, Calhoun thought.

Cool under fire and fearless, McCarter's torment came during the downtime. He was more comfortable in the field than garrisoned in a camp. That was like being in a prison to him, which led to his fearsome reputation for being reckless and for brawling with anyone who challenged him when the regiment was in Australia and New Guinea.

After the Noemfoor operation, Calhoun named McCarter a squad leader, but the promotion lasted only a few days. As the paratroopers waited for their next mission, McCarter disappeared. Rumors spread that he had made it to New Guinea, where he was fighting alongside some Australian units. That was never confirmed. But when orders came down that the 503rd was to attack Corregidor, McCarter reemerged on Mindoro, turning himself in to the military police. He wanted to go on the mission to Corregidor.

When Calhoun arrived at the stockade, McCarter was all apologies.

"I'm sorry," McCarter told Calhoun outside, after the military released him. "I'm sorry for the trouble I caused."

Calhoun brushed off the apology.

"It's no trouble," Calhoun said.

When they got back to the platoon, Calhoun put McCarter in third squad and returned him to his scout role. With the pending operation, he knew McCarter would be present and ready.

Plus, there was no way he was going into combat without McCarter's eyes and ears.

Scanning his men, Calhoun spotted George Mikel preparing his gear. Mikel, a former staff sergeant, had approached Calhoun a few days earlier with a peculiar request. Mikel was set to rotate back to the United States but refused because he wanted to stay in F Company. It was his home, he told Calhoun.

But Calhoun also knew Mikel had an unusual problem, because like every officer, Calhoun was forced to read and censor mail sent from his unit. Calhoun hated the job. But having read Mikel's mail, he knew the paratrooper had gotten an Australian woman pregnant and married her in Gordonvale without permission of the army commanding general.

The problem was the army didn't recognize Mikel's wife as next of kin. In the eyes of the military, his next of kin was his sister, Rose Caya of Lynxville, Wisconsin. So, Mikel didn't want to go home because he was doing whatever he could to send money back to his pregnant wife in Australia.

Keeping his jump pay was paramount.

"If I become a private, will you take me into your platoon?" he asked.

Calhoun didn't hesitate.

"Yes," he said.

Mikel was a talented mortarman and excellent soldier. Calhoun hadn't had an assistant platoon leader since Ball had left to take over the E Company's mortar platoon, so adding Mikel would give him an extra leader, even if he was a private.

With Calhoun on board, Mikel went to Bailey and asked him to reduce his rank and assign him to first platoon. Bailey refused. He couldn't do it without a reason. Undeterred, Mikel left camp for three days without authorization. When he returned and turned himself in, Calhoun approved his transfer to first platoon as a private. Calhoun made Mikel an extra runner, joining Pvt. Edward Thompson.

Calhoun had a high tolerance for men like McCarter and Mikel, who to most professional soldiers were troublemakers, because his path to the army wasn't much different from theirs. He was an officer, but he hadn't graduated from West Point like Colonel Jones. Calhoun started at the bottom and worked his way into command, volunteering first for the army and then for any job that put him in harm's way.

Born in Columbia, Mississippi, in 1922, Calhoun was the oldest of four kids—one sister, two brothers—who often looked after his younger siblings as his family moved from Maryland to Texas with stops in between. Calhoun's father, a Methodist preacher, used to run around on Calhoun's mother. The family would get settled in a town, only to have his father's extramarital affairs spoil everything.

They finally settled down long enough in Texas for Calhoun to graduate from De Leon High School in De Leon in 1938. Right after high school, Calhoun joined the Texas National Guard and worked as a wildcatter, drilling for oil in Comanche County. In 1940, with no money or steady job, Calhoun marched into the recruiting office on Barksdale Field in Louisiana, and joined the Army Air Corps. He was eighteen years old.

Calhoun wanted to be a pilot, or at least a gunner. Like many other aspiring pilots, he discovered that his color vision wasn't as good as he thought it was. So the army sent him to aircraft armament school in Denver, Colorado, instead. When he got back to Barksdale Field, he was bored. There wasn't much to do and he didn't want to work on planes. He wanted to be in a combat squadron. He was coming off guard duty in December 1941 when he heard the news that Pearl Harbor had been attacked. At dinner, he and his squadron mates listened to the radio reports about the aftermath. After dinner, they had a company formation. The commanders issued passes so the soldiers could go into town. Calhoun was told to wear his civilian clothes and have a good time, because it would be a long time before they'd wear them again.

The United States was at war.

But Calhoun didn't intend to spend the war at a Gulf Coast training command post. He and four of his friends volunteered for everything until they saw a notice for the Airborne. The army needed volunteers for parachute school at Fort Benning. Volunteering came with immediate orders and a fifty-dollar bonus. Jump pay was all the incentive most of the men needed.

Calhoun was a corporal, but when he transferred out of the Air Corps, his rank was reduced to private. After parachute school, he was assigned to Company B of the 502nd Parachute Infantry, part of the new 101st Airborne Division, before earning a commission at Fort Benning's Officer Candidate School and getting assigned to the 503rd. The training was hard, and every one of his men volunteered for the dangerous duty. But by pinning on jump wings, Calhoun knew he'd be fighting alongside men as determined as he was. He was a paratrooper now, a cut above. He would never let his men down.

A FEW DAYS before the jump on Corregidor, the men of the 503rd did an equipment check. A typical Airborne platoon is trained to drop into combat with everything they need to wage war and win. Paratroopers carried an array of guns. Riflemen had either the semiautomatic M1 Garand or the carbine, which was lighter and featured a folding stock so it was easier to carry during a jump. Scouts were armed with a Thompson submachine gun. Each platoon had two Browning Automatic Rifle (BAR) gunners. The large, heavy rifles offered more firepower in case of ambush. A .30-caliber machine-gun team usually accompanied a larger patrol. The machine guns were part of the three machine-gun platoons in the battalion Headquarters Company. One machine-gun platoon was attached to each company. A mortar team with a 60mm tube, demolitions men, flamethrowers, and bazookas might come along on bigger operations.

Most of the paratroopers were also armed with secondary weapons, ranging from .45-caliber 1911 automatic pistols to revolvers. Trench knives and bayonets were constant companions. Most of the paratroopers carried two or three hand grenades, either fragmentation or phosphorus or both.

The individual equipment list for the Corregidor jump was long, but provided each paratrooper everything he'd need to fight and survive for forty-eight hours.

The list included:

Helmet
Helmet lining
Coveralls
Web belts
Canteens, 2
Canteen cup
Medical first-aid kit (individual for every man)
Entrenching tool (optional)
Weapon—M1 Garand, Thompson Submachine Gun,
      Carbine, BAR
2 plasma units (for medics)
Medical Corps bag and aid equipment (for medics)
Ammo clips
Trench knife (optional)
Jump knife (a pocket jackknife to cut parachute risers)
Poncho
2 hand grenades (most men carry 4)
K-rations (2-day supply)

Once their personal gear was ready, the paratroopers packed equipment bundles. The heavy equipment—machine guns, mortars, and communications equipment—was broken down and placed in burlap sacks attached to parachutes so it could be kicked out of the door ahead of the men.

Captain Bradford was tapped to jump with the first wave so he would be on the ground to treat the wounded when Second Battalion arrived. Once on the ground, his job was to rally with the rest of the battalion's headquarters and set up an aid station in the massive, mile-long barracks on Topside. Bradford supervised the packing of six medical bundles with surgical instruments, drugs, and bandages. Once ready, the bundles were numbered and stacked with parachutes attached.

BETWEEN PREPARATIONS, BRADFORD kept his daily routine of a morning swim down at the beach. One day he returned to his tent to find his former tent mate waiting for him. The man had transferred to the Forty-Second Division, but when he heard about the jump on Corregidor, he came to wish Bradford luck. Before the war, his former tent mate had served on Corregidor. He described the massive artillery batteries, which could easily become bunkers for the Japanese defenders. He also described the good machine-gun firing lanes off Topside.

"If they have sense enough to develop them," the man added. "If they have, which I doubt, it's bad news for us. If they haven't, it's bad news for them."

"S-2 says there is less than a thousand defenders," Bradford said, S-2 being the regiment's intelligence shop.

His former tent mate shook his head. He expected the Japanese had a pretty good-size garrison there.

"No reason they shouldn't have," he said. "So, look out for counterattacks once you're down."

The man left with a final "good luck." Bradford cleaned up and went back to preparing for the mission. But his friend's warnings weren't far from his mind. Unlike the 503rd's own intelligence, his former tent mate didn't have the same confidence in the ease of taking the Rock.

THE DAY BEFORE the jump, fifty-six C-47s thundered above the 503rd's camp as they arrived at Hill and Elmore Airstrips, both built by the Australian construction crews Calhoun and his men had protected when they arrived on Mindoro. Later that day, Colonel Jones assembled the whole 503rd on the parade field in the late afternoon for a final formation before the mission. The paratroopers, dressed in coveralls, web belts, and jump boots, came to attention.

"At ease," Jones said, standing in front of the formation.

He took out a sheet of paper and read some brief comments sent from General MacArthur. It had been less than three years since MacArthur had escaped Corregidor under the cloak of darkness, then was whisked away to Australia, where he delivered his famous promise. "The President of the United States ordered me to break through the Japanese lines and proceed from Corregidor to Australia for the purpose, as I understand it, of organizing the American offensive against Japan, a primary objective of which is the relief of the Philippines," he said at the time. "I came through and I shall return." In October 1944, he had indeed returned, wading ashore on the island of Leyte following the American invasion. But the job wasn't done until he liberated every island and the capital city of Manila.

Standing in front of his men, Colonel Jones gave the order to retreat.

"To the Colors."

All that was left to do was jump.

Bradford watched the companies march off the field, marveling at the men around him. "Some are pure adventure-seekers hunting a thrill; some are uncompensated egotists and want to justify an inferiority complex by extraordinary performance; there are some superficial characters, fearless, reckless, and thoughtless, who thirst for the bubbles and froth of life; and there are some (though fewer) with exceptionally stable personalities whose inner natures yearn for heroic deeds," he wrote later. "Though the men scoff at our regimental song, its verses draw a true picture of the average man's mental attitude in the line 'I'm proud I'm allowed to be one of the crowd of the parachute infantry.'"

But a sadness came over Bradford when he realized some of the men on the field would be killed in the coming operation.

Many will not come back, Bradford thought. *Which ones, I wonder?*

BACK AT F Company's area, the tent city the paratroopers once called home was long gone. All that was left was the wooden framework of a few disassembled tents, plus a handful of tents still standing for the men left in the rear.

Calhoun finished packing away the gear he couldn't take with him. It would stay on Mindoro with the rear detachment. One prized possession was a bundle of letters from his wife, Sarah Joe. Calhoun kept them carefully arranged by date, and as he read each one again and again he would picture his wife's raven hair and green eyes.

Back in high school, Calhoun couldn't take his eyes off Sarah Joe. He knew she was out of his league, but that didn't stop him from asking her out. Sarah Joe was very popular, so he was shocked when she picked him. What Calhoun did to win her over is lost to history, but whatever it was worked, because after he completed his training at Fort Benning, they eloped in May 1943 in Clovis, New Mexico, where Calhoun's parents lived at the time.

After his wedding, Calhoun had to report back to jumpmaster school, and then his unit moved to Camp Mackall, North Carolina. Calhoun rented a one-bedroom duplex in Southern Pines, a small town near the base, and sent for Sarah Joe. He and his new bride had three weeks as newlyweds before he departed for the Pacific theater. He left Sarah Joe, dressed in a blue coat with a fur collar, at the Santa Fe train depot. Her gaze locked on him as he climbed aboard the train for Fort Ord and eventually a transport to New Guinea. He watched her through his tears as the train whistle sounded and the engine pulled out of the station.

They didn't say it.

But both knew there was a chance this was the last time he might see her. Every time he looked at his wedding ring, he wondered why she picked him. All he wanted to do was get back to her.

Calhoun finished packing away the letters and clasped a silver identification bracelet with his name engraved on it on his wrist. The bracelet had been mailed to him by his wife in a cigar box with camera film. Calhoun smiled as he looked at it. It surprised him that the bracelet had even reached him; thieves in the mail shop usually stole cigars and film.

With everything packed away, his focus shifted from home to his job and taking care of his men.

ANTHONY LOPEZ WENT over his equipment yet again. He was to make the jump hoisting a Browning Automatic Rifle, whose .30 slugs would add some additional firepower to his platoon, perfect for breaking up ambushes on jungle trails. Confident the powerful weapon was in perfect working order, he examined his pistol, checking that it was clean, oiled, and secure in its holster. Next he inspected his straps and made sure his ammo pouches were full. Two canteens were filled with fresh water, and into a small pack went some food, enough to last three days. By then, they'd have a resupply of provisions.

Every item was in its place, every detail accounted for. Lopez had been a paratrooper long enough to know that if a man wanted to survive a jump, he had to be prepared. He had started as the assistant gunner in his platoon, carrying ammunition. Now he was the gunner and an assistant squad leader. There was no way he was going to watch the war from the rear lines.

With everything ready, he joined the rest of his friends in second platoon for beer and a movie. Each paratrooper got six cans of beer. It was an event welcomed more than payday, or real meat in the mess hall. Just in case any of the paratroopers lacked motivation, before the feature the projectionist showed a newsreel about the fall of Corregidor, the Bataan Death March, and Japanese atrocities. The images of American soldiers surrendering to the Japanese were seared into their memories as they sipped their beer and tried to take their mind off the jump in the morning.

There was no thought that they might have taken their last bath in the Bugsanga River. That they would be buried in the same fatigues they had washed just yesterday. That their casket would be a mattress cover with the ends tied shut by bow knots. Combat soldiers don't usually dwell on such subjects. Most die in disbelief, and fear a mission's cancellation more than going into harm's way.

Captain Bradford watched from the outskirts. His thoughts went back to Harvard and a saying he and his teammates used to repeat.

"*'Tis beer, 'tis beer, 'tis beer that makes the world go 'round!*"

Bradford was scheduled to leave at five A.M. with the first wave, so he skipped the movie to try to sleep. He'd found some space in a tent used by men not going on the jump. Before turning in, Bradford jotted down some notes in his journal.

"We ought to begin a thriller-serial tomorrow which can be a basis for stirring movies in years to come," he wrote. "So I guess I'll hit the sack."

———

MOST OF THE paratroopers slept outside that night. Calhoun sat on his cot, thinking about the small landing zone and the possibility of strong winds pushing his men into the sea. He'd studied the aerial photographs. The bombardments had made the drop zone treacherous. Spearlike steel reinforcing rods from the concrete rubble and broken tree trunks jutted into the sky, ready to impale an unlucky paratrooper. The tunnels underneath the island were packed with explosives and gunpowder for the coastal batteries, making the whole island a bomb.

That night, Calhoun didn't pray for his safety. He prayed for his men, and for his own strength to lead them well. Somehow going into harm's way was preferable to boredom. They'd traveled around the world, thousands of miles from home, and the only way back was to finish the job by taking Tokyo and defeating Japan.

Corregidor was the next step.

CHAPTER 4

First Wave

CAPTAIN BRADFORD WOKE up to a flashlight in his face.

"Where is that damned cigarette lighter?"

One of the men in the tent where he'd borrowed a cot was searching through gear strewn around the floor. The flashlight beam cut through the darkness, shining on the faces of the sleeping paratroopers. The soldier finally found his lighter and stomped out of the tent, leaving a number of occupants awake and grumbling. There was no way Bradford was going back to sleep now.

He stepped out, and stood watching the flames of a gasoline torch whip back and forth violently between wind gusts. The fire was mesmerizing. But with each gust, a feeling crept into Bradford's guts, that deep understanding that what you want so much could be taken away by something outside of your control. Strong enough gusts would scuttle the airborne operation.

Back inside, Bradford pulled on his boots and gathered his equipment. After passing through the mess line, he choked down a spoonful of dehydrated eggs and some coffee and then got into formation with the other paratroopers on the first wave.

NEARBY, CHET NYCUM stood in formation, waiting to hear his name. He noticed everyone else in his company had jump boots. Nycum looked at his own feet. He was still wearing World War I leggings because the supply clerk didn't have jump boots in his size. For a second, fear shot through his body. Being different felt dangerous.

Is there some damn thieving supply clerk somewhere with small feet and a beautiful pair of Corcorans? he thought.

Then he heard his name.

"Nycum?"

"Here."

He relaxed. His mind went from his boots to the mission. It was just a parachute jump again, something he'd done in training and in combat already. After roll call, the paratroopers headed for the trucks.

The sound of the trucks' idling engines rumbled across the parade field. Captain Bradford climbed into the back of a waiting truck, and soon the convoy slowly rolled forward. Headlights cut through the darkness. The planks of the bridge over the Bugsanga River rattled as the convoy crossed. Soon, Bradford heard the crunch of gravel as the convoy made it to the highway, then continued on toward the airstrip. When they arrived, waiting soldiers directed each truck to a designated aircraft. They parked next to the metal-plated runway.

The C-47s were waiting. The paratroopers vaulted off the trucks and each grabbed a parachute from the stack. They slipped "Mae West" life preservers over their heads in case they missed the island and landed in the water, and then strapped their rifles into place. A paratrooper next to Bradford tossed his Mae West to the side after struggling with it for a few minutes.

"The hell with it," the paratrooper said as he jerked his crotch strap under his leg. "Might as well drown as wear this thing."

Nycum took a parachute from the pile and strapped it on. As he kitted up, his mantra was simple: "I'm ready. I'm ready. I'm ready."

The paratroopers were trained, step-by-step, to ensure safety. Each parachute came in a canvas kit bag. The first step was to fasten the leg straps and run the chest strap through the handles of the closed kit bag. Inside the kit bag went the paratrooper's musette pack, map cases, binoculars, and other gear. Carbines and M1 Garands were strapped, muzzle-down, to the para-trooper's right side. The rifle's stock was flat against the para-trooper's body and secured with a six-inch-wide belly band, which held the reserve chute. The band was threaded through the kit-bag handles and secured over the weapon. The reserve chute went over the kit bag so that it would not fly up and hit the jumper in the face.

Paratroopers jumping with a Thompson let the rifle's strap out and slung it over their neck so that the gun hung below the reserve chute. They jumped with their elbows on top of the stock and barrel so they could fire while descending.

With the last strap secured, Nycum could only walk like a

penguin, burdened with rations, ten twenty-round magazines, four grenades—two fragmentation and two phosphorus—a trench knife, and a utility knife. His Thompson submachine gun was slung diagonally across his body.

"I'm ready."

With all their gear on, each paratrooper was carrying an additional one hundred pounds. They rested in the grass near the plane, waiting for the order to load. All around Nycum, men overburdened with equipment smoked and joked and laughed. Some talked eagerly about the mission. Finally, Nycum's jump-master gathered his paratroopers together under the wing for a final pep talk.

"We have been picked by MacArthur to retake Fortress Corregidor from the Japanese," he began, speaking in the same cadence as a football coach rallying his team. "This is our special honor!"

When the speech was done, Nycum drifted away from the huddle, his mind on the horror stories he had heard about the Bataan Death March. In January 1944, the American government had released statements from military officers who had somehow managed to escape from Japanese prisoner-of-war camps in the Philippines, testifying to how prisoners had been brutally beaten, bayoneted, and even shot as they were marched toward captivity. Japanese trucks had driven over some of the soldiers who collapsed from exhaustion. Those who survived the march often died of starvation in the POW camps. Nycum's anger built into rage. Any thoughts of his own mortality were replaced by the serious task at hand.

Finally the order came, and the paratroopers waddled like olive-green penguins to the doors of the waiting C-47s. One by one, each plane's crew chief helped them up the stairs. With the jump now 100 percent certain, morale soared. Anyone watching the paratroopers' smiles and easygoing camaraderie might have figured they were going on leave in Honolulu rather than into the cauldron of combat.

Dawn was brightening the horizon as the C-47s came to life. There was an electrical whirring and then the planes' engines growled and kicked over. The pilots released the brakes and the planes started taxiing. The lead plane's engines roared one more time, testing manifold pressure, and it bounced down the steel runway until it lifted off. The jarring ride inside the fuselage instantly turned smooth as the tires left the ground and the plane climbed into the sky.

They were on their way to Corregidor.

The C-47s worked their way into three-plane V formations. P-47 and P-38 fighters patrolled the skies like sheepdogs protecting the air armada as it thundered toward the Rock.

WEDGED BETWEEN TWO fully laden paratroopers, Bradford somehow dozed as the armada soared north. The inside of the C-47 was cramped and hot. The paratroopers—two bobbing rows of helmets, Mae Wests, buckles, packs, and weapons—sat almost knee to knee, their reserve parachutes on their laps. Some slept, like Bradford. Others smoked. A few took off their helmets in the hot plane, resting them in their laps. The engines made talking difficult, and the few words passed between paratroopers were done at a yell. After an hour, the men grew restless. Uncomfortable in the parachute harnesses and the cramped seats, they extended their legs out into the aisle. Bradford woke up from his short nap and stretched his calves and wiggled his toes.

Over his shoulder was a window. Bradford craned his neck so he could see the silvery ocean through the glass. He pushed back his helmet and pressed his face closer, straining to see the tops of the waves. They crested in white foam, a sign the wind was stiff. Two American cruisers came into view as the planes hit the mouth of Manila Bay. Destroyers in the same flotilla were firing at Corregidor. Smoke and fire belched from their deck guns. Bradford imagined the sailors on the cruisers and destroyers looking skyward as the planes passed. A pair of B-25 bombers streaked past Bradford's C-47, heading for targets on the island.

Bradford could just make out Topside from the window as the first seven-man stick of paratroopers stood up and hooked their fifteen-foot static lines to a cable that ran down the length of the fuselage. The paratroopers didn't pull their parachutes. The static line did. When the jumpers exited the door, the static line unspooled until it went taut and pulled the chute strapped to their backs. Only in the event of a parachute failure did the jumper manually pull a red ripcord from the reserve strapped across his chest. American paratroopers were the only units to use a reserve chute. The British and other units had discarded it for extra ammunition or space so they could fit more jumpers in the plane.

Outside the window, the C-47 was over Corregidor. It was hundreds of yards of rough, broken terrain, pockmarked from days of shelling and bombs. Smoke rose from the hump of Malinta Hill, which sat between Topside and the island's tail. Bradford was staring at the island and missed the green light. The jumpmaster counted to six and the first seven paratroopers disappeared out the door.

The static lines rattled along the anchor cable as the plane banked and came around for another pass. Bradford saw paratroopers drifting down below the wings. Parachutes from other sticks littered the parade ground and golf course. Bradford didn't see any smoke or firefights.

Maj. Thomas Stevens, the regimental surgeon, took the jumpmaster's place in the door.

"I'm going to hold you to a count of eight; then we'll pitch the bundle, and you follow it," Stevens yelled over the engines and wind at the first jumper in the next stick.

Stevens and another paratrooper dragged the door bundle filled with ammunition and equipment into place. Bradford got up and hooked his static line to the anchor cable. He was the last man in the stick. The paratroopers made one last check of his equipment. He felt the grenades in his pouch. Checked he could reach the string to inflate his Mae West in case he ended up in the bay. His knife and pistol were secure.

OK. All set to go, he thought.

As the C-47 approached the golf course, tracer rounds from a Japanese machine gun streaked past the wing. The plane kept coming, ignoring the ground fire. Bradford watched the light near the door. It felt like hours until the red light switched over to green.

The bundle went out of the door first. A few seconds later, Stevens gave the order and the first man was out, then the next. Bradford followed, the stick hitting the door and dropping in the wind without hesitation.

He cleared the plane without issue and felt the reassuring tug of the risers as his parachute opened and slowed his descent. The noise of the engine faded and all Bradford heard was the wind. He scanned the area under his boots. Bomb craters and ruins. It looked like a giant had punched holes in the top of the island.

The paratroopers had jumped at four hundred feet, meaning they had only a few seconds in the air before landing. As he got close to the ground, a gust of wind blew Bradford toward the battered concrete roof of a building. The ground was coming up fast. He pulled on the risers of his parachute, collapsing one side and pulling himself in the opposite direction.

Once he cleared the building, Bradford let go of the risers and the parachute inflated again. He landed in the parade field's grass with his legs bent at the knee, his chin tucked, and the parachute's risers grasped with his elbows tucked into his sides. The balls of his feet hit first and he threw his body to the side to absorb the shock first on his calf before rolling onto his thigh and back.

Lying on his back, Bradford was reaching for the clasp to unhook his chute when a gust of wind inflated it again. He struggled to his feet as it dragged him ten feet up a slope. The parachute finally stopped pulling when it got tangled in a bush. Bradford popped the chest strap and slipped out of his harness.

Because the parachutes were hard to control, paratroopers

were trained to not land on their feet, but instead to roll like Bradford had. All around him paratroopers crashed down. To the untrained eye, the landings looked like men falling from the sky kicking up dust and brush as they rolled with the impact. Bradford looked up to make sure no one was going to land on him as he gathered up his gear and got his bearings before heading to his rally point.

The hard part was done. He was on Corregidor.

THE WIND WAS deafening on Nycum's plane as the jumpmaster opened the door. The first stick of eight stood up in preparation to jump. The jumpmaster poked his head out of the door to make sure everything was clear.

The light changed from red to green and seconds later, the first stick was gone. The plane banked to come back around. The next time the jumpmaster spoke in Nycum's plane was to give the order to get ready.

"Stand up and hook up."

Nycum snapped his static line onto the cable running the length of the plane.

"Check equipment."

He inspected his gear one more time and the gear in front of him. The man behind him gave Nycum's parachute a check.

"Count off."

"One OK."

"Two OK."

"Three OK."

"Four OK."

Nycum's breath was coming in short bursts. His heart was beating at a frantic pace. His gaze was fixed on the door. The red light came on. Then green. The world paused for Nycum. No one moved. Everyone was waiting for the jumpmaster's order to go.

Then, like a shot, the paratroopers raced toward the bright light of the open door. Nycum's hand was on the jumper in front of him until both were in the airstream.

After the jolt of his parachute opening, Nycum looked up into a full canopy. He floated for a few seconds, just enough time to get his bearings. The wind pushed him backward as the ground raced up to meet him. There was no time to adjust. Nycum landed hard on his back in a cloud of dust. He was in a crater. Before he could move, paratroopers from the battalion headquarters jumped next to him and helped him out of his parachute harness. Snatching his Thompson submachine gun from its case, he slid a magazine into the receiver and chambered a round. When he got to the lip of the crater, he spotted an American correspondent holding a camera. The man had filmed Nycum's landing, and he'd learn later the footage of him with his World War I leggings made it into newsreels about the parachute assault on Corregidor shown back in the United States.

With G Company assembled, Nycum, as a scout, led them a short distance eastward to take up positions overlooking the soon-to-be invasion beach. Topside was a rocky mess, with shell craters and the crumbling relics of the American headquarters and barracks. Nycum picked his way through the field of craters to the edge of Topside. The order was given to dig in. Nycum found a hole deep enough for cover near the edge of the slope of the ravine. When he peered over the side, Nycum spotted a paratrooper using his rifle as a walking stick, limping up the slope. With each step he jammed the barrel into the ground and pulled himself forward.

"Give me cover," Nycum said to the men around him.

He dropped his Thompson and scrambled down to the limping trooper. Nycum slipped underneath the wounded man's shoulder and helped him the rest of the way up the hill. Nycum deposited the paratrooper into a crater. He grabbed the man's M1 Garand and started to clean the barrel. As he dug dirt out, two men jumped into the crater next to them.

"What's your name, soldier, where you from?" asked one of the men, clutching a camera in his hands.

The men were Army Signal Corps photographers. Ten photographers had volunteered to make the jump with the 503rd. It was their job to document combat operations, often finding themselves in the same danger as the subject of their photographs.

Nycum ignored them.

Don't they realize there's a war on, and we're in the middle of it? he thought.

He went back to his position and took up his Thompson. From his perch at the cliff top, Nycum could see the whole invasion play out. Destroyers south of the island fired at the beaches. Closer to shore, a minesweeper ran paravanes off the side to cut the moorings of any submerged mines. Nearby, LCIs loaded with American infantrymen were gathering for the beach assault.

Nycum spotted an LCM—Landing Craft, Mechanized—with a series of mortar tubes pointed skyward racing toward the beach directly beneath where he was crouched atop the cliff. When it neared the shoreline, the LCM opened fire, the rounds headed for Nycum's position. He rolled into the hole near some broken concrete slabs and pressed himself flat against the dirt as the rounds hit with an earth-shaking explosion. Shrapnel whistled past him and clanked against the rocks and debris.

When the firing stopped, Nycum poked his head out of the crater. He saw an LCI ferrying soldiers from the Thirty-Fourth Infantry Regiment to shore. A flotilla of ships was moving around the head of Corregidor with more men and vehicles. Two LCMs carrying tanks hit the beach. As the tanks and a water carrier moved up the sand, there was an explosion. A mine smashed the tread of one of the tanks, rendering it immobile. The rest of the men coming up the beach kept moving forward. There was little resistance and soon the beach was covered with American soldiers pushing forward between Topside and Malinta Hill.

ON TOPSIDE, CAPTAIN Bradford moved toward his rally point. His mind drifted back to the meeting with his former tent mate on Mindoro. He had warned about Japanese defenses, and had speculated whether they had developed good firing lanes off Topside for machine guns.

"If they have, which I doubt, it's bad news for us. If they haven't, it's bad news for them."

The Japanese hadn't. It was bad news for them.

Their defenses had been set up to repel an amphibious invasion, and for the Americans even that was progressing on schedule. The Japanese hadn't planned on an attack from the sky. Had they kept firepower on Topside, the airborne assault would have suffered the same fate as the 1941 German attack on Crete. The German paratroopers arrived on the Mediterranean island under intense fire and took heavy casualties. They barely secured the victory, aided by a tactical blunder when Allied commanders abandoned the main airfield, fearing a seaborne invasion, instead of continuing to attack the beleaguered paratroopers. When the Japanese realized Topside was under an airborne assault, they tried to turn their guns on the planes. But most of the machine guns were far down the ravines and couldn't reach the planes flying above. As the attack proceeded, the Japanese did move some machine guns into position. The copilot of one C-47 was killed by ground fire, and a paratrooper received minor wounds while still in his aircraft, but he still jumped. The Japanese were never able to get a good concentration of fire on the planes.

Bradford heard the roar of engines as transports overflew the landing fields, leaving more parachutes in their wake. Mortars, ammunition, artillery pieces, and medical bundles in canvas containers with colored markers—red, yellow, blue—smacked the ground with a thud. Bradford zigzagged his way forward as he followed the rest of the regimental headquarters toward a large three-story concrete building that overlooked the parade field on Topside's north side.

Before the war, Mile Long Barracks, the world's longest military barracks, had been used for the billeting of American officers and enlisted personnel assigned to Fort Mills. Built by American engineers, it had been designed to withstand the all-too-frequent hurricanes that swept through the Philippines. In the last few weeks, the barracks had managed to hold up against most of the onslaught of Air Corps bombs and naval shells that had pummeled Corregidor in advance of the invasion. The building had a massive porch that encircled the second floor. An inner corridor ran the length of the building. The entire length of the building measured over 1,500 feet, which is less than a third of a mile long. But soldiers used to walk the length of the barracks from the third floor down, covering one mile. MacArthur's office and headquarters had been located in the building before he evacuated in 1942.

Bradford reached the barracks and huddled behind some cover with a group of paratroopers from the regimental headquarters. Nearby, he spotted "Rigor Mortis," a lanky medic who earned the nickname because of his lethargic manner, limping toward him. When the medic got to the group, he sat down next to Bradford.

"What happened to your ankle?" Bradford asked.

"I landed hard and sprained it," Rigor Mortis said.

But the medic hadn't had time to treat his own injury. As he hobbled his way across the landing field toward the barracks, he had treated half a dozen injured men. Now out of breath and nursing his throbbing ankle, Rigor Mortis waited with Bradford as a group of paratroopers gathered near the middle of the building. The paratroopers had no idea if any Japanese defenders were inside, but they weren't going to take any chances.

"Take your platoon, Sergeant, and ramshackle through that joint," the platoon's lieutenant ordered.

The sergeant split his dozen men into two squads. He took the first squad. A corporal took the other squad.

"I'll take this side," the sergeant told the corporal, nodding to the left of the barracks. "You go down the other way, and we'll meet back here in the middle."

Bradford watched the men creep into the barracks.

Inside, the sergeant and his squad worked their way down the hall, weapons up, each step measured. They scanned the ruins for any movement. The sergeant's squad reached the far end of the barracks without firing a shot. They turned back toward the middle of the barracks when Thompson fire rattled down the hall from the opposite end of the barracks. The sergeant and his squad hustled toward the sound.

The corporal's squad had come across three Japanese defenders at the far end. The squad's point man had spotted a Japanese soldier waiting at the corner of the outer corridor, and opened fire with his Thompson. The first enemy soldier was cut down by the burst. When the shooting started, the corporal came through from the inner corridor and fired his carbine, and a second Japanese soldier, hiding nearby, fell. The last Japanese defender, now trapped, tried to escape. One paratrooper missed with his Garand as the Japanese soldier scrambled into a nearby room. The paratroopers had him cornered.

The corporal waved the rest of the squad over. He could see the Japanese soldier through a break in the wall, squatting with his back to the paratroopers. He'd squeezed his head and shoulders into a cupboard, but it wasn't big enough to hide him.

"He thinks he's an ostrich," the corporal said. "Give it to him."

"No. Let's roust him out o' there," the Thompson gunner said.

"Give it to him, you sap," the corporal said. "He's probably got a grenade in there. Quit stalling."

The Thompson gunner opened fire.

When the sergeant got to the far end, he found the corporal grinning.

"We got three, Sarge," the corporal said.

As the paratroopers went in to clear the room, they found a grenade next to the Japanese soldier's body, but it was a dud.

"You never know what to expect of a Jap," the sergeant told the paratroopers, "except that whatever he does, you wouldn't expect it."

A few minutes after they had entered the barracks, the platoon poured back out. Paratroopers from the regimental headquarters rushed inside with their radios, telephone wire, and maps. The supply section took four rooms on the ground floor. They unpacked the equipment bundles and started to organize the supplies.

Water. Food. Ammunition.

By the end of the first day, they'd gathered up all the equipment bundles they could find, salvaged all the usable gear, and set up water and ammunition distribution.

Nearby, the operations section righted overturned tables and found chairs. They set up an operations room on the second floor, spreading out maps and tracking troop movements as reports came in over the radio. Company commanders came in to update their maps and get real-time intelligence on enemy movements and the location of friendly units. A blackboard kept a running total of Japanese killed. Hung on the wall was a photo of Gen. Masaharu Homma, the commanding general of Japanese forces in the Philippines in 1942, watching the paratroopers retake the island.

Next to the operations room, the communications section set up a bank of radios and telephone lines. They established links to the naval flotilla patrolling the waters nearby and the bombers overhead. Wire teams spread out and set up telephone lines to strongpoints on the perimeter.

The busiest section was in the center of the building, where the medics and doctors set up an aid station. A work party cleared debris from the rooms and scoured the barracks for bedding. They grabbed double-decker spring cots and created a hospital ward.

As soon as the medics could get a bed set up, it was filled. The wounded came in waves. Some limped, nursing sprained ankles or broken bones from the jump. Others arrived leaning on a unit mate's shoulders. The most severe came in on litters—some improvised out of any material the paratroopers could find. Broken bones dominated the injury list. Jaws. Legs. There were few bullet wounds. Bradford and the other doctors circulated around the ward checking dressings. Bradford splinted bad fractures and rigged up plasma bags to treat the more seriously wounded.

By midday, there were three hundred men in the ward. The regiment expected a 29 percent casualty rate. Despite hundreds of wounded, the rate hovered near 12 percent, with only 3 to 5 percent being serious injuries.

There were over a thousand paratroopers fit to fight.

And more coming.

CHAPTER 5

Stand in the Door

FIRST LT. BILL Calhoun, leader of F Company's first platoon, sat by the door of the C-47 with his head resting on a rivet so he could look straight down at the sea, waiting for the island to come into view.

He'd heard the first wave leave that morning from Mindoro. Now it was his turn. Before boarding the C-47, Calhoun had noticed on one of the planes a row of bullet holes running diagonally across the fuselage near the horizontal elevator, dashing any doubt they were headed into harm's way.

Just before takeoff, Calhoun met with the pilot. He'd just returned from dropping the first wave and wanted to brief Calhoun on the conditions over Corregidor. The wind was about twenty nautical miles per hour, the pilot said, and jumpers in the first wave were having trouble hitting the landing fields. He expected it to be about twenty-five nautical miles when they returned.

"I'm going to let you call the altitude," the pilot said. "We can go in between three hundred fifty and four hundred feet. Do you want me to go in at four hundred?"

Calhoun shook his head. "No, go in at three-fifty."

"Want me to drop down another fifty feet?" the pilot said.

Calhoun mulled it over. Getting his men safely to the ground was his primary job as jumpmaster. At that altitude, they'd only be in the air for a few seconds, but any malfunction could be fatal.

"Take her down," Calhoun said.

They'd be dropping at three hundred feet, but it would keep them out of the wind and give the paratroopers a better chance to hit the landing field.

Calhoun's men were in good spirits during the flight, laughing, joking, and smoking. Superstitions were going full bore. Some men wouldn't light a cigarette from the same lighter after two had already used it—an old belief among soldiers that by the third light, an enemy sniper had zeroed in on the kill. A couple of his men were nervous. Calhoun paused to give each one some encouragement before returning to his perch near the open door so he could see the lights.

When the red light near the exit door finally illuminated, Calhoun got to his feet. They were close. The mood in the plane changed. Cigarettes were stubbed out and the joking was replaced with action. Paratroopers put on their helmets, secured their chin straps, and prepared to jump. All eyes were on Calhoun as they waited for him to give the order.

"Get ready," he yelled. A moment passed, every man tense and waiting.

"First stick, stand up and hook up!" Calhoun shouted over the engines, making a hook with his index finger and moving it up and down as if he was snapping his static line into place. Eight paratroopers nearest the door got to their feet and snapped their static line to the cable.

"Check equipment!" Calhoun yelled.

One by one, the paratroopers checked to make sure the paratrooper in front of them was ready to jump.

Harness fastened.

Check.

Excess static line folded up and secured with a rubber band.

Check.

Static line in the jumper's right hand.

Check.

When the last man was done, Calhoun shouted: "Sound off for equipment check!"

Each man answered the command. Then Calhoun gave the final pre-jump command.

"Stand in the door."

The C-47s shifted from a V formation into two lines as they approached the island. The left line would pass over a big gun battery, Battery Wheeler, dropping paratroopers on the old parade ground designated Landing Field A. Calhoun's line, to the south, would pass over Crockett Ravine and drop paratroopers on the old pitch-and-putt golf course designated Landing Field B. The planes would circle back after the first pass and make two more, jumping eight men each time. Tech. Sgt. Philip Todd, Calhoun's platoon sergeant, led the first stick. Staff Sgt. Chris

W. Johnson led the second stick, and Calhoun would jump on the third pass with the last stick.

Calhoun and Todd slid the first bundle of mortar ammunition next to the right side of the door and then Todd took his position in the opening. The other seven men stood behind him as close as possible.

Calhoun rested behind the ammo bundle. He peered into the waters of the South Channel leading into Manila Bay. Hazy gray American cruisers and destroyers slipped under the olive-green wings as the plane thundered forward. The ships surrounding the island reminded Calhoun of the Indians attacking a wagon train in one of the Saturday matinees he watched as a kid. He was about to jump into the middle of Indian Country.

Todd slapped Calhoun on the shoulder as he adjusted the ammo bundle so that it sat on the lip of the door, making it easier to push when the time came.

"There it is," Todd said.

The cliffs of Corregidor rose out of the sea under the plane's wing. Calhoun could make out the green barrel of a 12-inch battery on top of the cliff. Then another. The island was bristling with guns designed to ward off ships.

As the C-47 crossed the shoreline, Calhoun spotted the deep ravines that ran off the bulbous head on the west side of the island. Calhoun saw olive-green chutes strung out from the sea all the way to Topside. They covered the golf course and parade ground. Calhoun spotted one chute down in a ravine.

As the plane got closer to the landing field, Calhoun heard the crack of rifle fire and the rattle of machine guns. He was searching Topside for the source of the gunfire when a 40mm round punched a grapefruit-size hole in the fuselage. Calhoun could see daylight coming through the hole. But the C-47 pilots never wavered. They leveled their wings and came in slow and steady so the paratroopers could exit safely.

For a second, Calhoun wished it weren't his job to make sure his men jumped on time. His mind was racing as he scanned the ground passing quickly underneath the plane, searching for his "go" point. He closed his eyes for a split second and willed himself to be calm. He'd easily landed in the circle during the practice jumps on Mindoro. *Trust your training.*

He opened his eyes in time to spot the "go" point—Belt Line Road—which cut into the cliffs near a ravine. He saw the ruins of the Officers' Club, another landmark from the aerial photos and the sand table, on the other side of the road, and then the swimming pool on the edge of the golf course.

The green light replaced the red light next to the door.

Calhoun started counting in his head as the plane thundered over the road: *One, one thousand. Two, one thousand.*

We're low, he thought.

Three, one thousand. Four, one thousand.

Keep cool, Calhoun told himself. *Don't hurry.*

Bang. Another round punched a hole in the plane.

Five, one thousand. Six, one thousand.

He shoved the bundle of mortar ammo out of the door. Todd replaced the bundle in the door.

Seven, one thousand. Eight, one thousand.

Calhoun slapped Todd on the leg.

"Go!" Calhoun yelled.

Todd disappeared into the wind. Less than a second later the next jumper hit the door. All eight were gone in a few seconds. The plane passed over the tadpole-shaped island and circled back for another pass. Going over the jump in his head, Calhoun worried he'd miscounted, forcing Todd to fall short. He prayed as he waited for the next pass.

"Lord, help me get these men down safely," he said as the C-47 started back over Topside.

PRIVATE LOPEZ WASN'T nervous as he dozed in his seat. He was a paratrooper. This was how he got into the fight. His mind was on getting the stick out the door and then finding his squad on the ground. He had never been a jumpmaster, and now he had to make sure an Army Signal Corps photographer jumped safely.

Back on Mindoro, Lopez had been donning his parachute when First Lt. Ed Flash, his platoon leader, came up to him. The squad was splitting in half and two correspondents—a writer and photographer—were jumping with them.

"You take the second half," Flash told Lopez. "You go six men back and you're going to be jumping out with a photographer with you."

Lopez looked skeptical. Before he could ask if the man had ever jumped, Flash cut him off.

"Make sure he goes out the door," Flash said.

"OK," Lopez said with a shrug.

The photographer had stood nearby as the two men spoke,

shooting photos as the paratroopers prepared to board the planes. Now, inside the C-47, he looked scared. But Lopez didn't have time to worry about him. He was worried about getting the stick out safely. All he knew about being a jumpmaster was when he saw the green light, go out the door.

Lopez was wrong.

The green light meant the pilot was at the landing field. He was supposed to count off before he exited. But when the green light came on over Corregidor, Lopez shoved the photographer out the door and followed. He felt the tug of the parachute and looked up to make sure the canopy was full. He had about four seconds in the air. More than enough time for him to realize he'd missed the landing field.

So had the photographer.

They drifted below Topside into a tangle of trees and brush. Lopez crashed into a tree and his parachute got caught in the branches. He slid down the trunk, the weight of his body and his gear pulling the parachute harness even tighter against his torso. Lopez struggled to free his arms and then reached for a pocketknife near his collar for cutting the riser lines. He groped for it but the parachute harness forced the knife under his chin. He tried to dislodge it, but couldn't. It was stuck, and so was he.

Jesus Christ, how am I going to get down from here? Lopez thought, thrashing about in hopes of dislodging his parachute.

All around him were the sounds of war. C-47s groaned above. Rifle and machine-gun fire echoed in the distance. Lopez felt like a target in the tree. He groped for the pocketknife again, but couldn't dislodge it. He tried to reach a trench knife in his boot, but it was too far to grip. All he could muster was his fingertips brushing against the hilt.

Then he heard someone coming through the brush.

Lopez froze.

Oh God, they're coming. They're coming for sure, he thought.

He reached down and pulled his 1911 .45-caliber pistol out of the holster on his belt and waited. The rustle of the brush got louder. Any second he expected to see the khaki uniform of a Japanese soldier emerging from the brush. Lopez leveled the pistol where he expected the soldier to come out, when an American helmet broke through the branches. It was the photographer, with his camera dangling around his neck. The man looked straight into the barrel of Lopez's pistol.

"Hey," the man said, raising his arms.

"Come on up and give me a hand," Lopez said, lowering the gun. "I'm stuck up here."

The photographer grabbed Lopez's feet and pushed him up, loosening the tension on the harness. Lopez freed the pocketknife and cut the parachute's risers.

"Thanks," Lopez said, picking up his BAR and equipment.

The photographer smiled.

Both men paused to get their bearings and headed off in different directions. Lopez never saw the photographer again.

OVERHEAD, CALHOUN'S PLANE was back over Topside and another stick and a bundle of supplies exited the aircraft. Calhoun stuck his head out of the door and watched the paratroopers descend. A gust of wind blew them off course, and his heart sank. He was sure they were blown out to sea. He'd killed Sergeant Johnson and the second stick, he just knew. Frantic, he was about to pull his head back into the plane, when he saw a stream of smoke. Up ahead, the engine of the lead plane was damaged. Instead of turning back for another pass, the smoking plane was headed back to Mindoro. Calhoun watched the smoke trail as the lone C-47 flew off. His plane made a sweeping turn and headed back for Corregidor for its final pass.

"Stand in the door!" Calhoun yelled over the drone of the engines.

It was his turn to jump. Calhoun leaned out of the door so he could see ahead of the plane just as his stick pushed up against him, making it hard for Calhoun to square his shoulders. He tried to push against the men behind him, but they wouldn't budge. The green light flicked on and Calhoun forgot about his shoulders. He counted nine seconds and stepped into the wind.

Paratroopers are trained to jump with their head down and feet together. Calhoun got caught looking back to make sure his stick was ready, and his left shoulder was ahead of his right. He was facing the engines instead of straight out when the wind hit him.

One second, he saw the engine. The next, he saw his boots against blue sky.

He was upside down.

Silk flashed by his feet and he felt the parachute pop open, jerking him upright again. The drone of the aircraft engine faded and for a few seconds it was just Calhoun and the wind. He looked down to get his bearings. Topside looked like a tornado hit it. Bomb craters. Snarled trees sticking up like spikes. The bombs had splintered the tree trunks into massive, deadly stakes, pointing like stiletto knives into the air. It was like jumping into a porcupine.

Calhoun heard the sharp crack of a passing bullet. It rattled his eardrums. Machine-gun fire thundered past him. He looked up at his chute to check its condition. The silk was riddled with holes. The ground was coming up fast when a wind gust caught him. His parachute started oscillating wildly. Calhoun aimed for a crater near the Officers' Club pool, but came up short. He smashed into a rock and then slid into the crater. A wind gust inflated Calhoun's parachute again and pulled him flush against the crater wall before bunching up against the rocky edge.

Calhoun was dazed. He came to as a couple of paratroopers helped him out of his harness. He tried to move and winced in pain. His right side was on fire. He took a deep breath and felt daggers of pain shoot through his chest. He'd broken ribs for sure, he thought. Calhoun took a second to let the jolt of pain fade to a dull throbbing.

He didn't have time to waste. Bailey expected him to get to the rally point. Calhoun snatched his musette bag and reached for his M1 Garand, but the rifle fell apart in his hands. The buttstock was shattered. He picked up the splintered rifle stock in one hand and the barrel in the other. Only the sling held it together. The rifle was useless and he tossed it away. He collected the rest of his gear and headed for the F Company assembly area. On the way, he took a working M1 Garand from a wounded paratrooper.

NEARBY, PRIVATE MCCARTER slipped off his harness and chambered a round in his Thompson submachine gun. Unlike Calhoun and Lopez, McCarter's jump was uneventful until he hit the ground. Soon after shedding his parachute, a bullet whizzed past McCarter's helmet. He scrambled for cover in a crater and scanned the area around him, looking for the source of fire. Another burst gave away the location of a machine gun thirty yards away.

Between him and the gun were a series of craters. McCarter waited for the gunner to shift fire to another target and then he crawled forward. Bullets peppered the ground around him. He rolled into a nearby crater as the bullets whistled past his head or ricocheted off the ground.

When the gunner again shifted fire to another target, McCarter crawled forward until he got to a crater close to the machine gun. The muzzle whirled back and bullets exploded around him as he slid into the crater and played possum. After a few seconds, he unhooked a pair of grenades from his belt and pulled the pin to the first one.

Then the other.

McCarter waited a beat. Then he tossed the first grenade into the machine-gun pit. The second grenade came close behind. McCarter pressed his face into the dirt and heard the muffled explosion as the grenades shredded the machine-gun crew.

After the explosion, the gun was silent.

———

CALHOUN HEARD INTERMITTENT firing as he made his way toward the last two-story house on Officers' Row. Officers' Row was built in the 1920s for the island's field-grade officers to live with their families. A broad street ran along the front of the houses lined with trees that offered some shade from the tropical sun. Parachute silk hung from some of the ruins, giving them a spectral look.

Calhoun stopped at 28-D, F Company's rally point. The company's mission was to defend the row of houses on this southern edge of Topside. First Lt. Bailey had selected house 28-D off of aerial photographs. The concrete house was still sturdy, with standing walls and two floors, but the roof had massive holes. Several shell holes in the yard facing Crockett Ravine to the south were quickly converted to fighting positions.

As Calhoun approached the house, he spotted Sergeant Johnson, who had jumped with the second stick, in a grove of trees talking to another paratrooper. Calhoun was relieved. He thought he'd sent the man to his death by jumping him too early. Johnson told him the wind blew him into the tall weeds at the edge of a ravine, but not over the cliff into the sea. Only eleven paratroopers from F Company were injured on the jump. No one died. It was the lowest rate in the whole battalion. Calhoun's ribs still ached, but he'd arrived with his platoon without losing a man.

Calhoun did a quick head count. His platoon was eight men short. His whole first squad. They'd been in the plane with the smoking engine that returned to Mindoro. He suspected they'd show up with the third wave the next morning.

LATE THAT AFTERNOON, across the parade field, First Sgt. Carl N. Shaw pulled a folded American flag from his pack. The command post at the barracks was set up, allowing Shaw, the top enlisted soldier in the regiment's Headquarters Company, to break away.

He called over Tech. Sgt. Frank Arrigo and Pfc. Clyde Bates. The trio made their way to the western edge of the parade ground. Shaw spotted an old telegraph pole out in the open. It was spiked for climbing.

"You fellows may be under a little fire," Shaw said as he passed the flag to Arrigo. "Hustle with the job."

Arrigo led the way, staying low to avoid sniper fire. Bates followed with some sound power telephone wire. Their mission was to get the American flag flying over Corregidor again.

The week before the invasion, the Service Company got permission to carry the flag on the jump. When Shaw got wind of it, he protested. It was Headquarters Company's job to carry the colors and Shaw went right to Colonel Jones, stopping only to chastise the Service Company on his way.

"You lowlife buzzards would steal the center pole out of the colonel's tent if you could get away with it," said Shaw, a tall, blond man who looked like a paratrooper from a recruiting poster. "But I'm telling you, you're not going to get away with it—this flag-stealing business. It's lucky I heard about it before you underhanded dogs had got the flags hid somewhere. You know blasted well that it's our privilege to carry the flag and always has been—and we don't have no notion to give it up."

The Service Company laughed off Shaw's threats.

"Well, don't let it get your gun, Sarge," said one paratrooper. "We don't have orders from the colonel yet."

Shaw met with the adjutant and then Jones, and when he left the command tent he had orders to carry the flag. He added it to his pack the same day.

"So no other skunks can make off with it," Shaw told Bradford when the doctor asked about the flag before the jump.

Now on Corregidor, Shaw and Bradford watched Arrigo and Bates zigzag their way to the pole. They scrambled up it using the spikes, reminding Bradford of monkeys climbing a tree. Japanese defenders zeroed in on them, rifle rounds cracking over their heads. Shaw and other paratroopers in the perimeter laid down covering fire, hoping to keep the Japanese defenders down. When they finally reached the top, Arrigo and Bates used wire to secure the flag to the pole. Then Arrigo tossed the flag into the wind and both paratroopers scrambled down. The breeze smoothed out the folds and the flag snapped into shape as the two soldiers rushed back to the perimeter unscathed.

After almost three years, the red, white, and blue with the stripes flew over Corregidor again.

CHAPTER 6

Battery Wheeler

AROUND 28-D, THE granitelike soil of Corregidor was proving too stubborn against the paratroopers' attempts to dig foxholes, so they soon turned to the existing bomb and shell craters to provide cover. While the men set defensive positions, Calhoun went inside the house looking for Bailey.

Inside, it was clear the Japanese had been eating breakfast when the first wave had swept in over the island. Calhoun spotted a *han-gou*—the Japanese mess tin—with rice on the table. The Japanese defenders had heard the bombs and then the C-47 transport planes and fled, leaving whatever they were working on or eating in suspended animation. Papers were scattered on desks. Filing cabinets were filled with documents. Of course, the documents were in Japanese and couldn't be read by the Americans.

It was as if the rooms were frozen in time.

A sergeant told Calhoun that First Lt. Bailey was at Mile Long Barracks meeting with battalion, so Calhoun went back outside. From the porch, he watched paratroopers running to rally points and forming up. Most military units enter battle in a cohesive group and combat scatters them. Not paratroopers. They enter scattered. But slowly, in small numbers, they gather into squads, then platoons, growing into companies and finally battalions.

While the rest of the company waited for Bailey, Calhoun decided to do a little recon of the area to get a better understanding of the terrain. He had a map, but nothing beat the experience of seeing the ground with one's own eyes. From the porch, Calhoun could see a massive coastal battery on the southwest side of the island.

"I'm going out toward that battery," Calhoun told his men as he started across the unkempt grass.

The terrain leading up to the battery was a flat yard the length of a football field. The ground was chewed up from the naval guns and Air Corps bombs. It was a moonscape of busted rock and dying vegetation. The ground looked like it had been tilled.

Calhoun stopped next to a railroad track—now just an overgrown bed after the Japanese had taken up the rails—once used to bring ammunition to the battery. He could make out the observation tower for the battery control station on the horizon. The square tower sat between two massive gunports, each home to a twelve-inch gun. The battery looked like a castle overlooking the South China Sea. Built on the site of an old Spanish fort, it was two stories of solid concrete, with thick walls built to withstand naval gunfire. Calhoun admired its strength. It was a marvel of American engineering.

As he got closer, Calhoun spotted a body in an American uniform. He recognized the man as Capt. Emmett Spicer, a doctor with the artillery battalion. He knelt next to the body and noticed an emergency medical tag hung from his boot.

Calhoun flipped the tag over so he could read it. It was filled out in full.

G.S.W. Perf. L. chest. Sev. (Gunshot wound, perforating the left chest. Severe.) Caused by Jap rifle fire. Corregidor, 16 Feb. '45.

Calhoun read the tag and saw the wound on the left side of Spicer's chest. He looked back at the tag. Under prognosis, Spicer had written "Death." Calhoun figured Spicer must have filled it out as he was dying. Calhoun took up his rifle and moved forward with caution. His eyes scanned the open windows as he got closer.

The first floor was the magazine and shell room. A pair of stairs met in an arc at the second level in front of each gunport. The top of the battery was covered by a layer of small slatlike boards. The gunports were a semicircle of concrete, with a massive pit where the gun rested when it wasn't firing. After it was loaded, the gun was raised over the parapet to fire and then retreated back to the pit where it was protected from counterbattery fire.

The guns, manned by a crew of twenty-two men, could fire thousand-pound shells almost ten miles. A Japanese bomber had disabled the traversing rollers of the number-one gun in March

1942. Although the crew managed to repair it, the gun was still difficult to traverse. The battery continued to fire until April 1942, when the Americans surrendered the island. Japanese soldiers used American prisoners to restore the number-two gun using parts salvaged from the number-one gun.

The railroad track that Calhoun spotted as he approached passed through the battery. A small hoist was set up over the tracks so the gun crews could unload the heavy shells from the flat cars and store them in the underground magazines below the battery. Calhoun figured the Japanese defenders were likely hiding in the tunnels just like the American defenders had three years earlier.

Calhoun approached carefully, his eyes going from the rooms on the first floor to the tower and back. Calhoun spotted some words painted in large peeling letters on the battery's wall.

BATTERY WHEELER
NAMED IN HONOR
CAPTAIN DAVID PORTER
CAPTAIN 22 US INFANTRY
APRIL 1904
WOUNDS RECEIVED IN ACTION

The word "infantry" was faded and almost gone. The last line was barely legible. A seventh line was covered by brush. Calhoun made note of the battery's name on his map. Calhoun's discovery was significant because the maps issued to the paratroopers didn't list the battery names. Instead, the paratroopers just called it the "big battery" until Calhoun found the name painted on the wall.

After peeking in the magazine and shell room on the first floor, Calhoun climbed up the stairs leading to the gunports. He noted how the high concrete walls tapered down to the ground. Small storage buildings and the latrine were built into the wall. A roof covered stairs heading to the second gunport. Calhoun inspected the open steel doors that led to the tunnel system used to bring up ammunition and gunpowder from the powder magazine.

Calhoun crossed over the middle of the battery to see the second gunport. Gunport number two was a copy of number one. Another set of stairs at the sea side of the gunport led to the top of the cliff that overlooked the South Channel.

But the battery control tower attracted the most attention. The tower joined the magazine at the rear. It didn't take a genius to grasp the tactical advantage the battery posed. The battery control station had a good field of fire over Topside. A perfect place for a sniper or machine gun. Calhoun was about to go inspect the tower when it dawned on him he was alone. If the Japanese were there—and in force—he was a goner. Calhoun beat a quick retreat to ground level and started back toward the command post at 28-D when he heard someone coming.

Calhoun took cover and snapped the safety off of his M1. He was prepared to fire, when the Second Battalion operations officer, First Lt. Lawrence Browne, walked out from behind the battery. Calhoun relaxed. Browne had just walked the length of the battery too, he said.

"There's nobody in this thing," Browne said.

They walked back past Spicer's body on their way back toward the parade field. Both men marveled at Spicer's commitment to order and procedure—even while dying, this military doctor did what protocol demanded.

When Calhoun got back to 28-D, Bailey was waiting for him.

Bailey told Calhoun to set up a defensive perimeter near 28-D facing Belt Line Road, a track that ran from Topside around the eastern edge of Cheney Ravine. The road was Calhoun's reference point on the jump. As the paratroopers dug in, they started to take intermittent fire from an old antiaircraft battery east of Battery Wheeler in Crockett Ravine, a steep V-shaped cut that ran down from Topside to the waterline.

Word came down from battalion that a squad of Japanese were firing at C-47s with an antiaircraft gun near Battery Boston, which sat south of 28-D and to the east of Battery Wheeler. It was down a slope from the parade field area across a field of craters. Thick jungle hid the Japanese movement as they attacked.

Browne, who'd just walked around Battery Wheeler, wanted Bailey to put a stop to it.

Bailey sent Calhoun.

"Clean out Battery Boston as quickly as you can, then go search the big battery for any Nips that might be hiding out in it," he told Calhoun.

Calhoun gathered his men and pushed out toward the battery. The whole platoon moved in unison like a single predator, with Calhoun as its brain. Even before the first shot, his undivided attention was needed to make sure the lead squads were headed in the right direction, the mortar crew was ready to support in the event of trouble, and he knew where to put the machine gun to cover an advance or withdrawal.

Combat was full-contact chess. Or as Bradford, an old Harvard football star, put it:

Each act depends on alert, quick-witted, cool-headed judgment; or, as a coach once expressed it on a football field, "Boys, keep your think-tanks pumping." There is hardly any task which can test a man's capacity in this respect as completely as that of leading a company in combat.

MCCARTER, THOMPSON SUBMACHINE gun on his arm, took the lead scout position as the platoon crossed the field of craters. Pfc. Richard Lampman, the second squad BAR gunner, followed closely. Calhoun was in third position, carrying his M1. The rest of the platoon, a bazooka team, and the mortar platoon's 60mm mortar followed. The paratroopers lagged behind McCarter as he danced across the battered landscape, picking out a path through the rocks and debris.

Up ahead, Calhoun saw McCarter stop. Then bound forward. McCarter charged forward on the balls of his feet, firing the gun in his signature style—flat against his forearm. The roar of his Thompson shattered the silence. McCarter raked the weapon back and forth, clearing out a crater before bounding forward again.

Calhoun charged forward. When he got to the crater, he found a Japanese machine gun and seven bodies. Up ahead, he heard the growl of the BAR. Lampman, closely following Mc-Carter, was closing in on another crater with his BAR against his hip. When a Japanese head popped up, he fired. As Lampman and McCarter advanced, the Japanese fired back. Both dove for cover in different craters. Before Calhoun could rally the rest of the platoon to move up and provide covering fire for the scouts, Lampman scrambled out of his crater and advanced into no-man's-land. The Japanese saw him coming. Bullets exploded around him as he worked his way toward them. Calhoun didn't have time to admire Lampman's courage, but watching him advance undeterred by the Japanese fire exploding around him would stick in Calhoun's memory for the rest of his life. When Lampman reached the edge of the Japanese crater, he opened fire with the BAR, killing seven more Japanese.

The patrol continued forward in this way. Each Japanese shot was answered by a maelstrom of American automatic gunfire. Crater by crater, the paratroopers cleared out the defenders. But each crater took them closer to Battery Wheeler.

Calhoun couldn't take his eye off the battery's east parapet. The battery had been empty when he was there with Browne, but he wasn't sure it had stayed that way, since the Japanese defenders were advancing up from the depths of Crockett Ravine. If they could get up the ravine close enough to fire on the command post, they could get to the battery too. If he were the

Japanese commander, he'd put some men in that battery to cover his flank. And clearing the battery and its thick concrete walls was much more difficult than sweeping craters. They could set up a hell of an ambush using the concrete battery like a bunker.

Calhoun called up first squad.

"I need you to clear that battery," he told Sgt. Bill Freihoff, the first squad's assistant squad leader. "Can't have the Japs on our flanks while we clear the rest of the ravine."

Freihoff selected Pfc. Albert Thomas, Pfc. Delby Huff, and Pfc. Glenn Hanlon, and together the paratroopers headed toward the parapet. Calhoun and the rest of the platoon continued to clear out the craters. They had made it a few hundred yards when Calhoun saw Thomas running from crater to crater to join him. Thomas slid to a halt next to Calhoun, his chest heaving. Thomas usually spoke slowly, but now the words flew out of his mouth.

"Lieutenant," he said, "Hanlon is dead. A Jap machine gun opened up and hit him. I think he's dead."

Thomas's squad had been approaching the rear of Battery Wheeler when a Nambu light machine gun in the concrete tower above the north parapet opened fire, killing Hanlon. Calhoun's hunch was right. The Japanese were in the battery and using the tower. It was a bigger threat to the command post than the ravine.

"Freihoff and Huff ran through a door into the battery," Thomas said. "I ran back by the big bank. But Hanlon is laying out in that open road."

Calhoun rallied his men and they headed toward Wheeler.

The platoon veered off the road and up onto a small hill covered in brush to the rear of the battery. It was the perfect place to set up an overwatch position so Calhoun could recon the battery and come up with a plan.

"Todd, Thomas," Calhoun said, signaling them to follow. He also signaled the bazooka team.

They crawled forward about thirty yards through the brush up to a berm near the crest of the hill and into a crater, where they could overwatch the battery. From the crater, he could see the number-two gunport and the commander's station in the concrete tower above the north parapet between the gunports. Thomas pointed out where he thought the Japanese machine gun was located in the tower. It sat either at the intersection of a concrete walk near the number-two gunport or near a four-foot wall on the battery's second floor. From either vantage point, Calhoun knew the Japanese gunners could see anyone approaching.

Calhoun called up the bazooka gunner.

"Fire at the walls in both positions," said Calhoun, pointing out the likely locations of the machine gun. The gunner shouldered the bazooka tube and the loader slid a shell into place and tapped him on the helmet.

The gunner aimed and fired. The bazooka sounded like a shotgun. The rocket raced out of the fifty-four-inch barrel and smashed into the reinforced concrete. Calhoun, Todd, and Thomas watched the battery, waiting to see if the explosion flushed out any Japanese defenders, but nothing happened. The crew fired over and over again until they were out of rockets.

The barrage had no effect and there were no signs of the Japanese, even though Calhoun knew they were in the battery. He also wasn't sure where Freihoff and Huff were trapped. He turned to Thomas.

"Where are they?" Calhoun asked, motioning toward the battery.

Thomas crawled up next to Calhoun on the edge of the crater and pointed to a door to the left of the parapet. Calhoun surveyed the door and then slid down to the bottom of the crater to make room for Todd, who climbed up to the lip of the crater to get a look at the door. He wanted to see where they were trapped as well. Calhoun was at the bottom of the crater waiting for Todd to finish so they could talk about an attack plan when the *thwack* of a bullet hitting steel startled him.

Calhoun looked up just as blood gushed from Thomas's mouth. His head seemed to droop beneath his helmet as his body went limp and he fell face-first into the bottom of the crater next to Calhoun.

Calhoun ducked to make sure he was below the top of the crater and reached down to check Thomas. He already knew the man was dead, but it was instinct more than reason. Calhoun spotted a hole in Thomas's helmet. It was in the back, not the front. Fear shot through him like lightning as he pressed himself against the side of the crater. The Japanese were in front and behind him now. He was cut off from the rest of the platoon and trapped.

Were they surrounded?

How many Japanese were out there?

Was the rest of the platoon about to get hit too?

Todd slid down next to Calhoun. He was shaken as well. Both men gripped their weapons as they slowly rose up and scanned the area, straining to see any sign of the enemy. The sun had set and it was dark and hard to see anything. Calhoun ducked back down. He didn't dare poke his head up again, but he also knew they couldn't stay put. No action was often worse than any action. Before he could give an order to move, the area behind the crater exploded in gunfire.

Frightened at first, Calhoun kept his head down until he realized it was American weapons firing. As the echo of the last shot faded, he heard his men call out, "We got 'em, Lieutenant."

Calhoun popped his head up and crawled back toward his men. Sprawled out in a spider hole directly behind the crater were the bodies of a dead Japanese officer and soldier. The blast of the bazooka had masked their approach. They had killed Thomas, but the sound of their shot alerted the rest of Calhoun's platoon, who came running. Free of the sniper threat, Calhoun told everyone to hold their position. He was going back to 28-D to get the flamethrower.

Calhoun worked his way through the brush to the road. He had taken a few steps down the moonlit road that ran parallel to the railroad tracks when a Japanese machine gun opened fire. Calhoun dove into a drainage ditch. When the firing stopped, he gathered himself and leapt out, taking off in a full sprint. For the next fifty yards, he alternated between dashing for his life and diving into the ditch. Each dash was met by machine-gun fire exploding all around him.

The firing stopped when he disappeared behind a curve. Calhoun was spent. He slumped into the ditch with his back against the incline and his feet dangling across the narrow opening. He was winded and closed his eyes to regain his composure. When his breath returned to normal, Calhoun climbed out of the ditch and headed toward 28-D. He was about to give the Divine a much-deserved thank-you when his world turned into a massive explosion. The concussion knocked him back into the ditch. His chest stung as a sharp pain shot through his injured ribs.

Calhoun crawled out of the ditch and stumbled forward toward 28-D. He ran his hand over his cheeks and forehead and felt something wet. In the darkness, he couldn't tell if it was blood or not. Calhoun started to panic. Oh no, he thought, his face was blown away. Rushing into 28-D's living room, where the headquarters was set up, he grabbed Bailey.

"I was hit by a mortar shell," Calhoun said.

Bailey turned on his flashlight and looked at Calhoun's wounds.

"Yeah," he said. "There's some scratches there."

But Bailey wasn't concerned.

"Nothing serious? Blood?" Calhoun said, his mind picturing his once-rugged face a mess of lacerations and puncture wounds.

Bailey shook his head. "No."

Calhoun exhaled and looked at his hands in the beam of a flashlight. Then he smiled. The wetness wasn't blood. It was sweat.

He finally calmed down.

"I came back for the flamethrower," Calhoun said.

Bailey had anticipated this and called a flamethrower team to 28-D just in case.

"They're here," Bailey said. "They're waiting outside."

"OK, you bastards, you had it, now you're going to fry," Calhoun said as he headed out the door.

He found the two-man flamethrower team in the grass near the house and headed back toward Battery Wheeler. Instead of using the road where he'd taken machine-gun and mortar fire, he led the men from crater to crater until they reached the hill. Then they crawled through the brush to the crater overlooking the battery.

Strapped to the flamethrower operator's back was the M1A1. The weapon's fuel tank consisted of two upright bottles. A smaller propellant tank was located between the fuel tanks. The nozzle of the weapon was located at the end of a long, thin pipe, which was connected to the backpack by a hose. The pipe was slightly bent and had a battery-powered igniter at the end. The flame ignited the fuel, which was forced out of the fuel tank through the hose.

Calhoun showed the operator where Freihoff and Huff were trapped on the first floor under the number-one gunport. Calhoun wanted the flames on the second floor of the concrete tower above the north parapet, where he suspected the machine-gun crew was hiding. The operator nodded and sprayed the fluid on the walls of the battery and pressed the igniter.

Nothing.

The operator hit the igniter again.

Nothing.

The flamethrower team crawled back from the lip into the bottom of the crater and slid the tanks off the operator's back. They inspected the tanks, the hose, and the nozzle. When they checked the igniter, it was damaged. It wouldn't fire.

"It must have been damaged during the jump," the operator told Calhoun.

The mishap probably saved some lives though. It dawned on Calhoun later that had he sprayed a flamethrower into an artillery magazine full of black powder, the explosion probably would have killed everyone.

Calhoun sat in the crater and racked his brain. His men were stuck. But it was dark now and he figured all he needed was some smoke to cover Freihoff and Huff's escape. Phosphorus would work. He called up a private with the only phosphorus rifle grenade in the platoon. The private screwed the rifle grenade onto the barrel of his M1 Garand as Calhoun yelled instructions to the trapped paratroopers.

"We got one rifle-smoke grenade," Calhoun told Freihoff and Huff. "We're going to fire it. When that smoke goes up, you all run for it. We're going to create all the disturbance we can."

The rest of the platoon set up on the ridge overlooking the battery and prepared to fire. The private aimed at the concrete tower above the north parapet and pulled the trigger. The grenade sailed into the battery and hit true. But nothing happened. No explosion. No smoke. Calhoun was dumbfounded. He looked at the private and then back at the tower. The private and Calhoun crawled down to the bottom of the crater and went back over what he'd done, step-by-step. Then it dawned on him.

"I forgot to pull the pin, sir," he said.

Calhoun shook his head. Everything was going wrong.

Calhoun was left with only one course of action. They were going to have to make an assault. Calhoun had wanted to avoid a frontal attack, but he was out of options. He was about to get his men on line to attack when he spotted movement to his left.

Staff Sgt. John Phillips and Private McCarter were sliding down the berm between the tower and the crater. Phillips, who had just got back from leave before the jump, had turned down taking over the mortar platoon because he didn't know anything about the weapons system. He wanted to be in a rifle company and floated between the platoons. As he and McCarter came down the berm, both paratroopers opened fire on the tower. Grenades followed.

"Over here, you fucking Nips!" McCarter shouted, keeping a steady stream of fire and expletives aimed at the Japanese. Phillips followed McCarter's lead. Both men kept pumping lead until Phillips ran out of ammo. He snatched up the carbine next to Hanlon's body and continued to pour rounds into the tower.

After the first couple of bursts, the Japanese machine gun answered back. Rounds chewed up the berm, forcing Calhoun and the rest of the paratroopers to duck down. The gunners quickly zeroed in on McCarter and Phillips, forcing them to take cover under the number-two gunport.

But the distraction worked.

Freihoff and Huff saw the shift in fire and made a run for it. They dashed out of the battery and made it down the road to the safety of the curve. Calhoun watched them go, and relief washed over him. He was never so glad to see anybody in his life.

But now McCarter and Phillips were trapped almost in the same place.

Calhoun brought the rest of the platoon on line with the crater and they opened fire on the tower. The suppressing fire kept the Japanese pinned down behind the battery's walls as McCarter and Phillips scrambled up the berm to safety. With everyone accounted for, the platoon moved back toward 28-D. The attack was a disaster and they'd lost two men with nothing to show for it. But when the last man made it back to the command post, the whole platoon felt a sense of relief.

They felt like they'd just won the war.

CHAPTER 7

Tiger Marines

PVT. TONY LOPEZ clutched his BAR and peered out of the window of the noncommissioned officers' quarters just north of 28-D, looking for a target. From outside the window he heard whispering in Japanese. Boots scuffed the gravel as men approached the two-story house.

It was only a matter of time before they attacked.

First Lt. Ed Flash's second platoon had set up in the noncommissioned officers' quarters for the night. The building was located just below the crest of where the southwest end of Topside descended into Cheney Ravine on the near side of the parade field. A number of paratroopers from Company E had landed short, ending up in Cheney Ravine. Japanese defenders were in the ravine attacking American positions on Topside. Colonel Jones and Major Caskey, the Second Battalion commander, were briefed on the situation, and Flash's platoon was sent to the noncommissioned officers' quarters to set up a defensive position and rescue any paratroopers trapped in the ravine.

Lopez spent the first day recovering bodies in Cheney Ravine. It was a slow and tedious process, not to mention dangerous. The paratroopers had to crawl under Japanese machine-gun fire to the dead troopers, cut them from their harnesses, and drag them to safety.

Lopez covered his unit mates with the BAR as they went out to recover their brethren. The paratroopers made every effort to recover the fallen, because the Japanese were known to mutilate bodies.

But as darkness approached, the Japanese became bolder.

They had already infiltrated Topside, twice forcing the paratroopers to flush them out. The Japanese harassed the Americans with sniper fire. They ambushed them from spider holes and congregated in the tunnels deep in the ravines waiting to counterattack.

American planners had accurately assumed the Japanese would focus their attention on the lower elevations, where they'd expected US forces to land by sea. Now dug in on the high ground, the paratroopers realized they had gaps in their defensive perimeter. There were some zones of interlocking machine-gun fire, and the mortar teams zeroed in on Topside's most obvious lines of approach, but the western side of the landing field facing Battery Wheeler was exposed. The side was too big for Second Battalion to cover, leaving a two-hundred-yard gap between Calhoun's platoon, now back at 28-D, and Ed Flash's platoon at the noncommissioned officers' quarters. A bigger gap was between Flash and E Company.

Lopez was on the first floor of the house facing the window, so he could fire out if the Japanese attacked. The building was set up like the officers' houses, with desks and chairs. Bags of rice and soy sauce in wooden buckets cluttered the room. Cooking utensils, clothing, and towels were thrown in a heap in the corner. Lopez heard the crunch of gravel under a boot outside again.

He searched in vain for any movement. The Japanese defenders were probing the lines on their way to Topside. Then Lopez heard a *thunk*, and he turned just in time to spot a grenade hit the floor. Lopez and the others popped to their feet and dove into a nearby closet filled with irrigation hoses.

The grenade exploded, shaking the house and blasting shrapnel around the room. As the dust settled, Lopez tried to stand up but was hopelessly tangled in the irrigation hoses. The paratroopers were told not to fire at night for fear of exposing their position. Once it was dark, paratroopers didn't move unless it was an emergency. But when Lopez got free of the hoses, he flicked off the safety on his BAR.

"Oh, this is crap," he said. "They already know where we are. Hell, we've been fighting each other all day long. They're going to kill us all before we even fire a shot at them."

Lopez walked toward the door leading to the second-floor balcony and shot a glance at his squad mates.

"I'm going to go out," Lopez said. "Don't shoot me. I'm going to get these sons of bitches before it gets us all killed."

Lopez reached the second floor and crawled out on the balcony. He could hear the gravel crunching below again and then silence. He moved his BAR into position and waited. A few minutes later, he could hear the Japanese soldiers talking to one another in a whisper.

Lopez hung the rifle over the side of the balcony and opened fire, peppering the gravel patch below. One of the Japanese soldiers screamed as the burst hit him. Lopez didn't stop firing. When he was out of ammunition, he pulled the rifle back. The ringing in his ears slowly faded into silence. He waited, listening for the crunch of gravel or the Japanese whispering, but it never came.

After a while, Lopez returned to his position inside the house and waited until dawn. As he sat in the dark, an uneasy feeling came over him. He'd been in combat before and knew the boredom and terror that came with it. One second, you're walking. The next, machine-gun fire is screaming over your head as you try to press your body flat against the dirt. But there was something else on the island he didn't like, but he couldn't put his finger on it. A darkness or foreboding. Lopez tried to force the feeling from his mind for the rest of the night, but every bump and every noise was treated like an infiltrating Japanese soldier. Each one was answered by sporadic fire.

ONCE DARKNESS OVERTOOK the island, the men settled into their fighting positions—some in fresh foxholes dug from the sandy, rocky soil, others in craters caused by the preinvasion bombing— and waited for dawn. Aggressive patrolling on the first day had uncovered various stashes of goods salted away in storerooms all over Topside. Sake, sherry, whiskey, and beer. All the popular brands, both American and Japanese, were present. One paratrooper remembered finding Suntory Scotch, a Japanese brand known as "the finest Scotch Whiskey available outside Scotland." Others found storerooms filled with San Miguel beer. The Japanese had looted Manila's shops and warehouses and sent the spoils to Corregidor to be shipped back to Japan.

But the ship never came.

Besides booze, paratroopers found other goodies. Another room was filled with white shirts—too small for the American paratroopers—and another had assorted bolts of fabric. One paratrooper found a room in Mile Long Barracks with bolts of Japanese silk. He cut a swath of silk and carried it all the way back to the United States to his wife, who used it to make a dress.

After a long day, some of the paratroopers around Chet Nycum produced liberated bottles of whiskey and sake from their musette bags. His company was dug in overlooking Black Beach at San Jose Point on Bottomside, where the Thirty-Fourth Infantry had earlier that day waded ashore. Once the beach was secured, Nycum's company had been ordered to keep on moving at around that same level toward the quartermaster storehouse on the eastern side of the island between Topside and Malinta Hill, where they could overlook the landing beach and provide cover for the seaborne troops.

There were some small warehouses at the end of a rail spur.

As Nycum approached one, his platoon leader, Lt. Gordon English, field glasses in hand, stopped to get a better look at the target. It was a long brick building with a loading area where soldiers could pick up blocks of ice. There were several big cargo doors and windows. It was stout and well constructed, despite suffering the onslaught of artillery and air bombardment.

English raised his field glasses to his face just as Nycum gave him a warning.

"You better take cover," Nycum said.

Shots rang out, and English fell to the ground dead, dropping the field glasses in the dirt. The paratroopers scrambled for cover. A sniper must have spotted the field glasses, a surefire indication the person holding them was an officer. Moving cautiously now, they worked their way closer to the storehouse, when Nycum came upon an ammunition dump on a hill above the building. Shells were stacked up and wired with explosives. Nycum and the other paratroopers beat a hasty retreat and called headquarters. A demolitions team came and inspected the shells. The safest thing to do was blow them in place. They set off the ordnance in a thundering explosion.

Now, at dark, the men took long pulls from the liberated bottles and passed them on, up and down the line. Nycum took a few swigs. He found a shot of whiskey chased by sake made for a good mix.

Between shots of booze, rounds from the ammunition dump fire cooked off, sending shells tumbling into the air. The shells as they flew through the sky made a *kalk-kalk-kalk-kalk-kalk* sound, which reminded Nycum of wild turkeys. After a while, some of the paratroopers started shooting at the "turkeys" as they flew overhead. But word quickly came down to knock it off.

Don't waste ammo.

IN THE AID station, Captain Bradford and the other surgeons had made the rounds in the ward one last time before dark. Everything seemed in order. The stream of casualties from the morning was over. Darkness covered the ward like a blanket.

Medics tended to the patients after the doctors' rounds, stepping between beds and around weapons. Most of the wounded paratroopers kept their rifles close, ready to take on an infiltrator or beat back a banzai charge, if one broke through the perimeter.

All around them the sound of combat echoed and then waned. Like an accordion gathering air and then *boom*, an explosion of fire—rattling machine guns, the thump of mortars, and the sharp crack of rifles—and then a lull.

The silence was the hardest.

"I seen my own squad set up the perimeter just behind this building," Bradford heard a sergeant with a broken leg tell the patients around him. "Just so you boys can sleep easy."

Sporadically, someone would call out in a whisper, "Ward boy."

A medic would shuffle along the floor, feeling his way through the darkness. But most suffered in silence. Soon it was too dark to see anything. The wounded were left with the pain. Darkness brought isolation. A time when a wounded man's psyche was most vulnerable. When only he could grapple with the pain of a broken limb or a gaping hole in his body. When he was faced with his own mortality.

"That was the toughest night I ever put, Captain, it near run me crazy," a soldier told Bradford the next morning as the doctor changed his bandages.

ACROSS THE PARADE FIELD, Calhoun was dozing in his foxhole in 28-D's yard when he was jarred awake by screams.

"Help! Help!"

Pfc. John Jackley was yelling nearby. Calhoun popped his head up and saw two men rolling on the ground. He couldn't make out who was who. A couple of other paratroopers gathered around, their weapons at the ready. Before any could fire, Jackley got the upper hand and drove his trench knife into the other man's chest.

Jackley rolled off the dead Japanese soldier. His chest was heaving and his hands were shaking.

"What happened?" Calhoun asked.

"Something was poking me in the ribs," Jackley said as he regained his composure.

When Jackley had opened his eyes, he saw someone standing over him with a long pole. Jackley grabbed the pole, which had a bayonet wired to the end of it, and yanked it down. The Japanese defender fell into the crater and they started to grapple on the ground. Fortunately, Jackley had managed to get ahold of the trench knife and end the fight.

The next morning, Calhoun and his men crawled out of their holes only to find a number of Japanese corpses scattered about the front yard of 28-D. None of them carried rifles. Instead, the paratroopers found five-to-six-foot-long, one-inch-diameter steel rebar spears with one end sharpened or wood poles with a bayonet wired to the end.

Calhoun noticed some of the defenders had different uniforms. The color was nearly the same as the Americans' fatigues, with an anchor insignia on the collar. The helmet was missing the normal star. Instead, there was an anchor. They were Japanese Imperial Marines sent to the island in October 1944 to occupy ten 150mm naval guns. Under their uniform, they wore a wide silk band that was wrapped around their body.

Gold thread outlined a tiger. Calhoun started calling them tiger marines.

CHAPTER 8

Blood Brothers

LOPEZ WOKE UP the next morning covered in flies.

He shook them off and created a dust cloud. Dust covered everything. Ponchos. Packs. Weapons. Lopez looked around at his unit mates. After one day, the paratroopers' fatigues were filthy and caked with salt rings. But the flies were new. He hadn't noticed them when he first arrived on Corregidor, but now they covered everything. A sour smell hung in the air. Lopez knew it from past battlefields. Rotting bodies of the dead from the day before were baking in the sun. The flies arrived with the smell.

Lopez shooed the black swarm away with his hand. For a few seconds, the flies disappeared. Then they were back, crawling on his arms and face. He shooed them again and opened a tin of biscuits.

A brief reprieve.

Then, like mini kamikazes, they swarmed again, crawling on his hand and on his food. He shook them off and choked down the dry biscuit in a few bites, washing it all down with a swallow of water.

Lopez sloshed his canteen around, gauging how much water he had left. Everyone was rationing their water. They'd jumped with two canteens, but now most of the guys were down to their last couple of swallows. Everyone was thirsty and the water resupply still hadn't shown up because the Japanese blockaded the road to the beachhead. Water was dropped that morning in the resupply, but it hadn't made it out to Lopez's unit. Some of the men found some stagnant water in the bottom of the broken water tanks on Topside, but Lopez didn't drink it. He'd wait for the resupply.

FIRST LT. ED FLASH, Lopez's platoon leader, was near a cooking fire having breakfast when a guard started shooting.

"Hey, you guys, come look at this!" someone yelled. "You won't believe your eyes."

Flash and the others looked up. Coming down the road was a sporty red 1938 Ford roadster. None of the men knew it, but the car had been brought to Corregidor by a US officer in the years before the surrender. Now this most American of automobiles was being driven down the road with a Japanese marine behind the wheel. Two men were beside him, and three more passengers huddled in the back. Other Japanese were running alongside, trying to grab on and jump in. They were making a mad dash off Topside to the relative safety behind their own lines. The paratroopers were mesmerized. They hadn't seen an American car in years, much less a sporty red one jammed with

Japanese marines. It looked like a clown car crammed full of elbows and knees.

But there was nothing funny about it.

Before anyone reacted, a long burst from a .50-caliber machine gun near Topside's parade ground shook them out of their stupor. Bullets smashed into the side of the roadster, punching massive holes through the thin steel. The roadster skidded off the road and burst into flames. The paratroopers, now out of their daze, shouldered their weapons and opened fire as the Japanese marines piled out. The fusillade cut down the survivors before they could escape into the brush.

The incident affirmed what the paratroopers knew: the Japanese were hiding in the caves in the ravines running from Topside down to the water. At some point, they knew the Japanese would come for the high ground.

AFTER BREAKFAST, LOPEZ and his squad took up a position at the edge of Cheney Ravine. All morning they'd glimpsed flashes of tan uniforms in the ravine below—Japanese marines running across from cave to cave. Lopez figured the Japanese radios were knocked out, because there was no other reason for them to be running one or two guys back and forth unless they were delivering messages.

After watching a few cross, he shouldered his BAR.

"Don't let them across," Lopez told his squad. "Knock them down. Knock them down."

When the next runner appeared, the Americans opened fire.

The first rounds hit nearby and the runner picked up the pace. He zigzagged as rounds exploded all around him. He was about to get across the mouth of the ravine when he finally crumpled to the ground in a hail of fire.

They cut the next runner down too.

The echo of the last shot was fading when someone spotted another runner.

"There's one, there's one," called one of Lopez's squad mates.

Lopez scanned the ravine and spotted a man waving his arms. He was wearing an American uniform. The paratroopers were about to open fire when Lopez shouted.

"Hold it, hold it," Lopez said. "That's not a Jap. He's got one of our uniforms on."

"That's a Jap," one of Lopez's unit mates said. "They're just trying to fool us."

The man in the ravine took off his helmet and Lopez spotted blond hair.

"That's not a Jap," he said. "That's one of our guys."

There was no way they were going to leave him to the Japanese. Earlier that morning, a patrol near Battery Wheeler found a dead paratrooper still in his harness, the body horribly mutilated with bayonets. Lopez called Flash over to his position. The man was likely wounded, or he would have tried to make it up to Topside. Flash took one look and turned to his platoon.

"You guys cover us," he said. "We'll go get him."

It was Staff Sgt. Leonard LeDoux. He was one of a number of paratroopers from E Company who had fallen short of the parade field. Flash and Pfc. Angelos Kambakumis took off down the hill. Lopez watched them half run and half slide down. Flash and Kambakumis didn't take weapons or a litter.

How the hell are they going to carry the guy? Lopez thought. *Two guys can't carry a wounded guy up that rocky ridge.*

Flash and Kambakumis weren't halfway down when Lopez heard a burst of gunfire and both paratroopers dropped. Lopez and the others fired back, covering Flash and Kambakumis as they scrambled back into the brush. Lopez was anxiously watching the pair pick their way up the path to the top of the ravine. As they broke out of the brush, Kambakumis was holding Flash's left arm. Kambakumis had a big crease on the top of his head where a Japanese bullet had taken his cap off.

Flash didn't stop and headed straight toward the aid station. Lopez watched Flash walk off. *We can't leave the guy down there,* he thought. He turned to his friend Pfc. Bob O'Connell.

"O'Connell, do you want to go with me?"

O'Connell didn't hesitate.

"Yeah, I'll go with you," O'Connell said. "We've got to get him out of there."

Lopez scanned the area. He wasn't going to make the same mistake as Flash.

"We have to have something to carry him on," Lopez said.

Lopez and O'Connell dashed back to the noncommissioned officers' quarters and tore a bedspring off the wall.

"We're not armed, you guys cover us," Lopez said to the squad as he headed into the ravine.

———

FLASH PASSED THROUGH Calhoun's perimeter cradling his arm.

"What are you doing here?" Calhoun asked as his friend approached.

"I got shot." Flash showed Calhoun two holes in his left fatigue sleeve just above the elbow. He pulled up his sleeve and Calhoun saw a hole in his arm three inches above the elbow. The exit wound was on the back side of his arm.

"Got hit trying to drag LeDoux out of Cheney Ravine," Flash said.

The sound of American machine guns rattled in the distance. There was a firefight near Cheney Ravine as Lopez and O'Connell made their way down into it, so Calhoun made Flash wait at his position until things quieted down.

Sitting in the crater outside 28-D, Flash closed his fingers into a fist.

"See, I can clench my fist but I can't spread my fingers," he said.

When the shooting stopped, Flash got to his feet and walked across the parade field toward the aid station. Calhoun watched him and took solace that at least he could still walk on his own.

A little later, Captain Bradford came over to 28-D.

"How long will Ed be gone?" Calhoun asked.

Bradford shook his head. "Ed won't be back," he said. "That bullet severed the radial nerve. Ed is facing several operations and at least a year in the hospital in the States."

Another officer gone from F Company. Red LaVanchure, the

company executive officer, was in the aid station too with severely sprained ankles. The company had three officers left: Bailey, Calhoun, and Second Lt. Clinton D. "Sleepy" Miller, the mortar platoon commander.

LEDOUX WAS ABOUT 150 yards down into the ravine. Lopez and O'Connell, lugging the bedspring, slid down the steep cliff face and into the brush, slowly working their way toward their wounded comrade. When they approached the spot where Flash had been hit, they dashed across quickly to avoid any enemy fire.

When they reached him, LeDoux was lying in the brush barely conscious. Lopez noticed he was hit and couldn't stand. It must have taken the last of his energy when he signaled for help.

"We're going to get you out of here, buddy," Lopez said. "You're going to be all right. You're going to be all right."

O'Connell and Lopez helped LeDoux onto the bedspring. Lopez looked back up the hill, envisioning the route to safety. The Japanese were farther down the ravine. He couldn't see them, but he knew they had clear fields of fire on the only path leading down from Topside. Lopez also knew they'd be exposed on the trail, just like Flash and Kambakumis had been, but then he spotted a cluster of rocks to the left of the opening about twenty yards above them.

"When we get to the opening where the lieutenant and Kambakumis were hit," Lopez said, "go like hell because they're going to pepper us. When you get to the opening go to your left, where the high rocks are, and they won't hit us there."

O'Connell nodded his head. "OK," he said.

They stood and picked up the bedspring stretcher. With O'Connell in the lead, the pair scurried through the brush. Just before they reached the opening, O'Connell hesitated.

"OK," O'Connell said, "I'm going to go up."

O'Connell took one step into the opening and the Japanese machine gun fired. Bullets ricocheted off the rocks and kicked up the dirt. Lopez felt something bite into his left hip and burn. Seconds later, a bullet hit O'Connell in the back of the thigh.

"I'm hit," O'Connell said, crumpling to one knee.

Bullets continued to rain around them. Lopez saw LeDoux twitch on the stretcher as bullets hit him. Adrenaline shot through Lopez's body. They needed to move or die.

"You got to go," Lopez shouted to O'Connell, pushing the bedspring forward. "Go, you can't stop here now. You can't stop here."

O'Connell got the same jolt of fear. He jumped up and kept digging into the ground with one leg and pulling up the stretcher. Lopez pushed from the back as O'Connell finally made it to the high rocks. Under cover, they collapsed. Soon, they heard their platoon mates coming down the hill.

Both men could hardly walk.

A medic met Lopez at the top of the ravine. He wrapped Lopez's hip with two white pads and sprinkled some sulfa powder over the wound to ward off infection.

"Yeah, you got nicked pretty good," the medic said.

Looking at their injuries, the medic joked that the same

bullet took them out. It went through Lopez's hip and ended up in O'Connell's calf.

Lopez looked at O'Connell.

"Man, after that I'll call you my blood brother," he said.

O'Connell, who couldn't walk, was helped to the aid station with LeDoux. But LeDoux wouldn't make it to the aid station. He died on the way.

Lopez stayed with the platoon. He shook off his wound and fell in line as his squad moved down into the ravine to check on some tunnels.

The tunnels ran under the green hills and each opening was a possible exit point for the Japanese defenders. The paratroopers checked the openings and then, about three hours later, returned to their position overlooking Cheney Ravine. By then, Lopez couldn't walk. He reached the top of the ravine and slumped down in the grass. He called over the medic.

"Take a look. It doesn't feel too good."

The medic opened up Lopez's pants to look at the wound. It was red and swollen.

"You've got blood poisoning," he said. "You'd better get to the aid station. I can't do nothing for that."

Lopez got to his feet. He was in a daze, focused on just putting the next foot forward. He saw the aid station up ahead, and then nothing.

CHAPTER 9

Mail and Water

CHET NYCUM AND his unit mates woke to throbbing headaches and dry mouths. They'd spent the night dug in near the quartermaster storehouse on the eastern side of the island. While they were thirsty the night before, the thought of drinking more sake or whiskey turned their stomachs. Now, they just wanted the throbbing in their heads to stop.

Nycum was shaken from his stupor by someone calling his name.

"Hey, Nyk! Look at this."

Nycum joined a small group near the wreckage of a truck. A few paratroopers had used it for shelter. It was just a shell with no bed and pockmarks all over it. The Air Corps no doubt strafed it several times during the bombardment. When Nycum got to the truck, he spotted a Japanese defender lying in an ungainly tangle of limbs on the road.

"Whose trophy is this?" Nycum said, staring at the corpse.

It was the first dead Japanese Nycum had seen on the island.

"He took him with his knife," a paratrooper said, pointing at the company medic, who was standing nearby.

"I don't understand why he came to me to help him commit suicide," the medic said, cool and collected.

The paratroopers laughed nervously.

So far, Nycum and his unit mates were kept out of the action. After a quick breakfast, Nycum found himself again back on top of the ridge watching landing craft ferrying men to Black Beach. The beach was already busy with soldiers and supplies coming and going. From his perch in a crater near the edge, Nycum spotted a destroyer cruising near the tail of the island. It was covering a landing craft heading for the beach. As the landing craft got close, a Japanese heavy machine gun opened fire. The gun was about two hundred feet below Nycum's position. Bullets kicked up a stream of water in front of the landing craft as the gunner walked the stream of fire toward the target. Nycum saw sparks where the bullets crashed into the ramp.

Sailors on the destroyer spotted the machine gun too, and Nycum saw white water churn at the stern of the ship as it steamed into firing position. When it was parallel to the beach, the guns started to turn and face the machine-gun nest. That's when it finally dawned on Nycum what was happening. The ship was going to fire and he was only a couple hundred feet above the target. The Japanese hadn't come close to killing him, but it was the second time he'd been in the navy's line of fire.

Nycum didn't wait for the first shot to see how accurate the navy gunners were. He rolled away from the ridge and into a nearby crater. He tried to lie as flat as possible. He heard the roar of the destroyer's guns and then a deep, guttural rumble. It felt like the whole island shuddered. The destroyer's guns fired several volleys, pounding the machine-gun nest numerous times even after the Japanese stopped firing.

Finally, when the constant pounding was almost unbearable, silence.

Nycum crawled to the edge of his crater. Below him, the cliff face was smashed like someone had taken a giant hammer to it. With the threat done, Nycum continued watching the Thirty-Fourth Infantry arrive. An LCI was just landing at the beach. The ramp came down and a single man ran off. He stopped in the sand and waited for the rest to follow. From the cliff, he looked alone. Vulnerable. The only target for a sniper looking for an opportunity. For a second, Nycum felt scared for the man.

I don't know who he is, but he is one of the bravest men I have ever seen, Nycum thought as the man waited for the rest of the soldiers on the LCI to come down the ramp. *As dangerous as being a scout might be, he can have that job, I'll not trade. It's still better to jump from a plane.*

IT WAS SHORTLY after dawn on the second day when Captain Bradford saw the Red Cross director come into the aid station. There was a mail plane on the way, he said. Bradford and some of the other paratroopers from the headquarters ran out to the parade field. A few minutes later, Bradford heard the faint rumble of an engine.

Most of the paratroopers on the ground were expecting the First Battalion to arrive by airplane that morning. But Colonel Jones canceled the third jump, instead bringing in the First Battalion by LCI. With Black Beach secure, it was easier and safer to bring First Battalion in by sea because the Japanese lines were so close to the paratroopers, and the third wave wouldn't have the security of American bombers to soften the target. Jones didn't want to give the Japanese gunners a chance to shoot down a C-47.

But First Battalion didn't receive Jones's order until they were already putting on their parachutes. Instead of unpacking their ammunition bundles, the C-47s delivered them with the mail while the paratroopers flew to Subic Bay, where they boarded LCMs for Corregidor.

Back at the parade field, the drone of the engine grew louder and louder until Bradford finally spotted the green-skinned C-47 coming over the sea from the west. It was flying low as it crossed over the cliffs, heading right for Topside. When it was over the parade field, the pilot dipped the left wing and a bundle tumbled out of the door. The parachute caught the wind and the bundle slowed and floated to the ground. As the paratroopers ran to retrieve it, Bradford kept his eyes on the plane. The crew sergeant gave the paratroopers a wave before they banked and flew back the way they came. Other planes followed, bringing First Battalion's door bundles filled with ammunition, heavy weapons, and food. But for the men on Topside, the mail was the most important bundle to retrieve.

There are few things more important to a deployed soldier

than mail. Mail was more than ink and paper. It reaffirmed the connection to home and that the soldier was loved.

"This war has planted the outpost of the American home all over the world from Greenland to Burma, from Persia to the Aleutians, and all points between," Bradford wrote in his journal later. "Now once again those good, brave people back home, those moms and dads, and wives, and sweethearts and friends had found their place with us on the battle-crested summit of smoking Corregidor."

After the mail drop, Bradford returned to his patients until he heard, amid the intermittent gunfire outside, the pounding of a motor. It wasn't the far-off buzz of a plane. It was the deep, almost guttural growl of a truck or tank engine.

The Thirty-Fourth Infantry Regiment had secured the beach and were slowly clearing the middle of the island. A few hours before, Maj. Thomas Stevens, the regimental surgeon, sent two paratroopers down a concrete staircase that went from Topside to the beach. They avoided Japanese patrols and made it to the beach, where they organized a relief column with medical supplies, plasma, and water for the aid station on Topside. The beachhead had opened a vital lifeline of supplies, especially water for the paratroopers.

The rumble was getting louder as Bradford went to the window to see what was coming up the road. He spotted an open-topped M7 self-propelled gun, a mobile artillery that looked like a tank, with a short, stubby main gun and a pulpit-like machine-gun ring behind it. Built on an M4 Sherman chassis, the M7s were built to provide artillery support and keep up with tanks during armored attacks.

A pair of M7s landed on Black Beach with the Thirty-Fourth Infantry, but one was lost when it hit a mine. The lone M7—which the men nicknamed "Sad Sack"—stopped in front of the aid station and Staff Sgt. Bill Hartman, wearing a big grin, popped his head out of the cupola.

"Is this the 503 CP?" Hartman asked, using the military jargon for command post.

"You bet it is," Bradford heard a paratrooper say as they approached the guns.

The sound of the M7 drew a crowd. Paratroopers nearby huddled around the guns, talking to the crew and searching for supplies.

"Did you bring any water?" one of the paratroopers asked.

Hartman pointed to a stack of five-gallon cans piled on the back and sides of the M7. Some of the containers were still full. Others were lighter, having taken a few bullets on the way to the command post. The road from the beach to Topside was still contested, as evidenced by the armor scarred from Japanese machine guns.

Stevens, the regimental surgeon who sent the two runners down to the beach, came out of the aid station.

"Was it a tough trip coming up here?" Stevens asked.

"No, sir, Major," Hartman said. "We just crashed through and kept our heads below the armor without trying to fire back. They gave us a shower or two, but we made it all right."

Bradford and the other doctors had kept the wounded comfortable, but there were a few cases that needed medical attention they couldn't provide at the aid station. One patient had a badly broken jaw. Another was shot through both arms and paralyzed, and one had a compound ankle fracture after falling off a barracks roof. Three cases were growing more serious. One paratrooper had suffered chest and head wounds, and was barely conscious. Another had a neck wound, the swelling threatening to cut off his airway. The last patient got shot in the right arm. The blood vessels were damaged and Bradford feared he'd need an above-the-elbow amputation. Stevens wanted to move them to the beachhead so they could be evacuated to a nearby hospital ship.

"The fellows are absolutely helpless," Bradford told Hartman. "Do you think we should take a chance with them?"

Hartman nodded. "It's a safe enough ride," he said. "We'll only run through the Jap fire for half a mile or so on the downgrade. Beyond that, we'll reach the perimeter of the beach party, and on the way the Jap ambushes are as much as a hundred yards or more from the road. They can't come out in the open and rush us, even if we get stuck."

Bradford chuckled to himself. He thought it was funny Hartman considered a mad dash through Japanese ambushes a safe ride.

"Is the road rough?" he asked.

"It ain't smooth," Hartman said with a smile. "But there's no roadblocks."

"OK," Stevens said. "Bring those six wounded men out. They're not getting any better up here."

The medics brought the wounded men out one by one. Bradford tried to make them comfortable as they were loaded into the back of the M7. The wounded paratroopers were quiet, their lips tight and their jaws clenched as they gritted out the pain.

When the last one was on board, the engines roared to life and the M7 rolled down the uneven road toward the beachhead. Bradford stood in front of the aid station watching the precious cargo leave. He'd done the best he could. They needed better care, but he hated to see them go. These were his men. The guys he promised he'd care for in combat.

Now, he worried.

Would they get through? Would the ride make their wounds worse?

Five minutes later, Bradford heard Japanese machine guns open fire just as Hartman predicted.

"Well, they've got that far," one officer said to Bradford on his way back into the barracks.

It was the kind of comment Bradford was used to hearing. This was combat. There were no guarantees. The paratroopers on the line knew any day it could be their turn. Bradford knew the reality all too well, for when a paratrooper had his worst day, he ended up in front of Doc Bradford—assuming he made it that far. And hopefully Bradford was having a good day and saved a life. Back inside the aid station, Bradford continued with his duties, but the six wounded men were never far from his mind. Finally, late the next day, he got a report. They'd made it to the beach. After that, he never got another update.

WHEN THINGS WERE quiet in the aid station, Bradford liked to climb up on the roof of Mile Long Barracks. From this post, he could see the whole island. To the west was the South China Sea, like a piece of glass stretching blue and calm to the horizon. To the north he saw the tip of Bataan Peninsula across the North Channel, the dark hulk of Mount Bataan in the background. To the east, the tadpole-like tail of Corregidor. From the rooftop, Malinta Hill looked like the arched back of the giant tadpole. About a quarter of a mile south of the tail towered Caballo, a steep island that was part of the same ancient volcano that created Corregidor.

Looking down the length of Corregidor, Bradford watched the heavy shelling from artillery and naval gunfire as the Thirty-Fourth Infantry Regiment clawed forward, expanding its beachhead. Mortar shells exploded in small flashes. White smoke snaked into the clear blue sky from phosphorus grenades only to mingle with the black smoke and dust cloud caused by dynamite closing tunnel entrances. When the grenade exploded, it showered an area with a chemical that continuously burned unless deprived of oxygen. The chemical agent burned anything it touched, cloth or skin. Phosphorus grenades were used for smoke screens and to root out Japanese defenders in bunkers and caves.

In the waters around the island, US Navy cruisers and destroyers ventured in close to shore, their deck guns belching fire as they mauled Japanese positions. Bradford watched one cruiser become engulfed in thick black smoke as its guns unleashed a barrage, flames shooting from the barrels. Nearby, PT boats cut white wakes through the glassy seas. They maintained a constant ocean patrol around the island, cutting off the possibility of any Japanese escaping by raft to Bataan.

Above the island, the Air Corps dropped bombs and strafed the enemy with their machine guns. Once, he watched as a pair of silver P-38s dove toward Japanese positions. Red tracers flashed from the planes' front guns. The attack left Bradford's ears ringing as the P-38s banked and then climbed for another attack. Over and over again, the fighters, like birds of prey, dove at their targets.

But noise from the strafing attacks was minimal compared to the bombers. Bradford strained to pick up the planes against the blue sky until they were already descending to deliver their payload, especially the incendiary bombs. He watched one bomber release a pair of incendiary bombs that seemed to disappear in the brush. Then he saw a spark, and the brush went from a dull green and brown to a rolling wave of orange fire and thick black smoke. Seconds later, the bellowing of the explosion finally reached Bradford.

It was rare to come up and not see some kind of fighting. On the days he got to watch the battle, Bradford's mind drifted back to school and the writing of Homer. Sitting high above the action, he felt like a Greek god gazing down from Olympus over the Trojan battlefield. But his was a modern battlefield, a spectacle that would have left Homer awestruck. From the machine guns to the tanks, the might of the American military machine wasn't lost on Bradford. Hell, he'd jumped from a plane and landed safely on Topside, a feat that was unthinkable when the island fell three years before. His wasn't the old American Army looking to plant a flag on the world stage. No, it was a modern war machine able to attack by air, land, and sea anywhere in the world.

A couple of days after the jump, Bradford caught sight of a convoy of supply ships heading for Manila Harbor. It was the first relief convoy since the city fell three years earlier. The moment wasn't lost on Bradford.

"How many lives, what infinite suffering, and what a colossal mobilization of forces had been necessary to bring these few laboring ships to shore?" he wrote later. "The agony was over at last. America was returning, not as Dewey's great fleet came to take over a colonial possession, but with new, far-sighted visions of liberation and friendship."

CHAPTER 10

Inferno

THE BIGGEST CONCERN for F Company was Battery Wheeler. The massive coastal fortification that stood on the western end of the island still posed a formidable threat. Despite their successful rescue of Freihoff and Huff, First Lt. Calhoun knew the Japanese occupied the battery, and that the observation tower gave the enemy clear fields of fire across Topside.

Since the paratroopers landed, they'd been harassed by sniper and machine-gun fire. The specter of snipers was a constant in the back of the paratroopers' minds. A well-concealed shooter could wreak havoc on a unit, tying down dozens of men, each too afraid to move for fear of exposing themselves.

That morning, the western end of Mile Long Barracks was the scene of a terrific firefight. The roar of machine guns woke the staff, including Captain Bradford and Colonel Jones. Rounds smacked off the concrete as the Japanese poured fire into the building. Jones, with one of his staff officers, went to see the fighting. As Jones headed for the western end of the barracks, the staff officer protested. All around him, paratroopers were lurking in the balconies or along the walls waiting for a Japanese target to appear.

"Colonel," the staff officer said, "you shouldn't come out here. We don't know which way the Japs will be firing, but they sure as heck will be aiming at anyone they see go through here."

Jones had a reputation for being everywhere, so the paratroopers weren't surprised to see him heading toward the sound of guns. Second Lt. Flash called Jones the "General Patton of the Pacific Theater."

"You could always see him right in the middle of the action, helping wherever and however he could," Flash wrote later. "He marched with us on the trails and even helped the troops carry equipment."

Jones ignored the staff officer's warning and worked his way to a vantage point where he could see the action. Perched behind a wall, he watched as paratroopers stormed a nearby building just below the barracks and mortars hammered a house where some Japanese defenders were hunkered down. The staff officer, feeling safe next to the colonel, ventured a look closer to the edge.

"The Japs were just firing in here ten minutes ago, sir," one of the paratroopers said, still using the wall as cover.

The staff officer laughed.

"Well, I guess they're gone now," he said, looking over at Jones. "Colonel, I guess neither of us is much good on taking cover."

———

THE JAPANESE PLACED a high degree of importance on marksmanship. In their military, being a good shot was not a specialty but the norm. Their training was of sufficient intensity that the average Japanese infantryman was as good a shot as a sniper in other armies. Of course, the Japanese units on Corregidor were varied—many were left over from the Shinyo suicide-boat units, some were sailors from sunken ships, some were even construction workers. Many didn't even have rifles. The Japanese marines on Corregidor were the best shots and the backbone of the defense. Their favorite aiming point was the forehead—dubbed "bore-sighting" by the paratroopers.

The day before, a Japanese soldier had snuck into some demolished buildings near the barracks. Finding a perfect perch to hide in the ruins, he zeroed in on the headquarters and began squeezing the trigger of his rifle, masking his shots with the sound of combat on other parts of the island. The paratroopers didn't notice it until they heard the whine of ricocheting bullets.

"The son of a bitch must be shooting at us," one of the officers said, ducking down to avoid the soldier's sights.

Bradford, back from visiting Calhoun, found cover behind concrete railings or doorways. The paratroopers cussed the sniper until a squad showed up to find him. They searched the surrounding buildings but came up empty-handed.

"We must have gotten him with one of our machine-gun bursts," the squad's sergeant told the headquarters staff after his search turned up empty.

But a couple of hours later, a paratrooper was visiting his friend in the aid station when he doubled over in pain. Blood gushed from his side, and he fell to the floor in agony. Bradford and the medics converged on him. No one had heard the shot, but it had to have come from the same direction as the sniper.

"How about that," one of the medics said to Bradford in passing. "He comes in from the perimeter and gets wounded in the hospital."

Bradford smiled at the gallows humor. But the sergeant in charge of the squad who failed to find the sniper the first time didn't see any humor in the attack. He gathered up his squad again and restarted his search.

"I'll [get him] if I have to pull those buildings down on top of him," he said.

The squad searched for a half hour. They thrashed through the wrecked houses around the aid station but again turned up nothing.

BACK AT 28-D, Calhoun could see into Battery Wheeler's number-two gunport. If the Americans could see it, then the Japanese hiding inside could certainly see the command post at Mile Long Barracks. The only way the paratroopers could hold the southwest side of Topside was to root the Japanese out of the battery, which wouldn't be easy.

American engineers had built the battery to withstand an assault from both naval guns and aircraft. The paratroopers had tried to get a pack howitzer in place on the porch of 28-D to shell the battery, but the crew couldn't depress the barrel low enough because of the concrete rail. The only way to neutralize the Japanese inside was for troops to take the battery.

"Campbell is preparing to assault Battery Wheeler," Bailey told Calhoun. "Want to give him the layout?"

Lt. William Campbell was a replacement. He had joined the 503rd only a few weeks before the jump, taking over third platoon. Two days before the Corregidor mission he got some good news. His wife had given birth to a son.

Calhoun wasn't happy about the planned attack. Battery Wheeler was formidable and he'd already lost two men there. There was nothing in Wheeler worth taking. Better to just destroy it so the Japanese couldn't use it.

"Why not bomb it?"

Freihoff and Huff told Calhoun there were big canisters of black powder in the room where they hid. One napalm bomb would set off the black powder and smoke out any defenders.

Bailey shook his head.

"No," he said. It was decided that after a heavy shelling with the 75mm, the platoon would assault.

Battery Wheeler was thick concrete built to withstand fire from ships at sea. What was a pack howitzer going to do? Nothing. Just like the bazooka.

"You're crazy," Calhoun told Bailey. "Suicide."

But an order was an order, and Calhoun met Campbell when he arrived at 28-D. The officers sat down around the map. Calhoun sketched out the battery, showing Campbell the berm where first platoon took cover the first day and the location of a bunker behind the battery where he could set up. He told Campbell he could get close to the battery there, and then attack. As the meeting was breaking up, Calhoun had one more piece of advice.

"Raise your head to look," he said. "Then move. Japs like to zero in on a place when they see a head. They'll wait for it to reappear. They're patient."

Campbell gathered his map and got with his platoon. Calhoun and Bailey took up a position on the second-floor porch and watched the paratroopers move out down the dirt road toward the battery. A few minutes later, the soldiers started up the stairs that led to the top of the parapet. Calhoun let out a cheer as they made their assault, then automatic fire smashed the silence. From his place on the balcony, he could see five men tumbling down the battery's stairs. It was too far to see if they were Japanese or American.

"Was that our guys?" Calhoun said to Bailey.

Was that the third platoon attacking? Did they just watch their own guys get killed?

Both Calhoun and Bailey became physically sick until word came back the men were Japanese killed by an American machine gun, but that didn't ease their nerves.

Both officers were getting impatient. The attack was risky, but waiting didn't make it less so. If the Americans were going to take Battery Wheeler, it would call for swift, decisive action.

After the first burst of fire, no more shots rang out. Calhoun and Bailey were still waiting for an artillery barrage when the first soldiers from third platoon came running back down the road. Soon, the rest of the unit was following.

The whole unit was in a panic.

Calhoun and Bailey dashed down to the first floor of the house and met the platoon as they got to 28-D. The platoon sergeant was the first man back.

"What happened?" Bailey said.

Platoon Sgt. Joseph Shropshire was rattled. He could barely talk, his breath coming in heaves. When he finally calmed down, he gave his report to Bailey. The platoon had moved down the road and set up on the berm just as Calhoun suggested. Campbell and Second Lt. Dorval Binegar, the commander of the demolition section, took up a position in a concrete bunker in rear of the battery. The whole unit was lined up, ready to rush over the berm and assault the battery. Campbell told Shropshire the battery appeared unoccupied and ordered him to tell the men to fix bayonets. As Shropshire worked his way down the line passing word, Campbell and Binegar each raised their head up in the same place as they had the first time, checking their target, yet disregarding the advice Calhoun had given. One second the officers were talking about the approach to the battery. The next both men went limp, Japanese bullets taking their lives.

By then, the attack was under way. Shropshire took command and gave the order. Several phosphorus grenades were thrown, and under a cloud of smoke, Shropshire and the rest of the platoon charged toward the battery. A pair of Japanese machine guns opened fire, scattering the charging paratroopers. Shropshire tried to flank the guns, but he was pinned down. The machine guns stalled the attack and Shropshire ordered his men to throw more phosphorus grenades and pull back using the smoke for cover. He led the men away from Battery Wheeler with four men carrying the bodies of Campbell and Binegar.

When the sergeant had finished, Bailey looked at Calhoun. He was angry about Shropshire's withdrawal. They'd made it halfway. Not pressing the attack only forced them to go back and attack an alert enemy. There was no way to regain the element of surprise. The aborted attack had also cost Bailey two officers at a time when he needed leadership. F Company's mortar platoon commander, Lt. Clinton "Sleepy" Miller, had been hit by machine-gun fire earlier that morning. The company was now down to Bailey and Calhoun.

"Get the third platoon back out there and get ready to attack," Bailey told Calhoun.

Calhoun got his gear as the third platoon squad leaders gathered the men. It took about a half hour to organize the platoon and lead them back through the brush and into position behind the berm.

"We're going to use WP grenades to provide a smoke screen," Calhoun told the men. "Then we'll rush number-two gunport."

Calhoun could see on the faces of the men that they didn't want to do it. The Japanese were waiting for an attack. The paratroopers had just watched their commander die. They knew Freihoff and Huff got trapped there on the first day and Hanlon had been killed nearby. This was a suicide mission, even with a smoke screen to hide their approach.

But Calhoun also knew there was no other way. The concrete battery had to be taken. Calhoun paused to gather himself. Maybe he said a little prayer for his men and for help leading them. But during the pause, a runner from 28-D came down to the berm.

"Hold on," he told Calhoun. "D Company is coming down to attack."

Calhoun pulled back and headed to the command post. A new mission was waiting.

"What's the plan?" Calhoun asked.

Bailey ordered Calhoun to take his platoon and reoccupy the area around Battery Boston, which he'd patrolled earlier that day looking for a sniper. The battery was east of Battery Wheeler. His platoon would support the left flank of the assault on Wheeler by Lt. Jimmy Gifford from D Company. Artillery was going to put smoke rounds on the battery before Gifford's men attacked.

"You can't put artillery on that with us so close," Calhoun said.

The howitzers were sitting on the parade ground, and they wouldn't be able to get enough arc in such a short space to hit the battery, Calhoun said. Instead, the rounds would sail over the target and land in the sea.

But Bailey dismissed Calhoun's concerns. It wasn't up for discussion. Calhoun got his platoon and set off toward Battery Boston. The platoon slogged through the crater field and through the mangled brush. It took about thirty minutes to get to the battery and set up a hasty perimeter near the guns. Calhoun found a vantage point from which to watch the artillery bombardment.

The thunder of the pack howitzer echoed across Topside.

Calhoun, using his field glasses, watched the shells sail over the parapet and slam into the sea. He shook his head. There was no smoke in the battery. Instead, the smoke was billowing over the water several hundred yards off the coast.

Gifford's men had no cover now, so they went to plan B. They'd been supplied with hand and rifle phosphorus grenades, and the men started bombarding the battery. Soon, a thick white smoke hung around the concrete structure. The smoke was so dense it was impossible to see the paratroopers on the berm.

"Follow me!" Gifford yelled, and led his men toward the battery.

Calhoun's men opened fire from the berm, hoping to keep the heads of the Japanese down as D Company paratroopers headed for the number-two gunport.

Calhoun lost sight of the paratroopers as they rushed into the smoke, and he ordered his men to cease fire. From his position near Battery Boston, Calhoun heard the barks of rifles and machine guns, and then, as the smoke cleared, he saw Gifford lead his men to the top of the magazine, where they met a wave of Japanese marines with bayonets and fists. The two units collided like ancient Roman legionnaires, hacking and slashing at one another in a massive scrum. For several minutes, the hand-to-hand fighting raged until finally the paratroopers overpowered the Japanese. When the fighting stopped, the bodies of sixty-three Japanese marines littered the battery's two gunports.

D Company controlled the outside of Battery Wheeler.

No doubt there were Japanese defenders in the tunnels below the battery. But the Americans controlled the high ground.

COURTESY OF PAUL WHITMAN

COURTESY OF PAUL WHITMAN

Throughout his punishing days of combat, Calhoun's young bride, Sarah Joe, was never far from his mind.

At the age of only twenty-two, First Lt. Bill Calhoun was already a veteran paratrooper who had earned a Purple Heart by the time orders to take Corregidor were handed down to the men of the 503rd Parachute Infantry Regiment. During the battle, he led F Company's first platoon. Here he holds a Thompson submachine gun.

COURTESY OF PAUL WHITMAN

Capt. Charlie "Doc" Bradford parachuted onto Corregidor during the first wave and set up an aid station in Mile Long Barracks on Topside.

COURTESY OF PAUL WHITMAN

Pvt. Tony Lopez *(back row, third from left)* was an assistant squad leader and BAR gunner from Colorado. He served in F Company's second platoon.

COURTESY OF PAUL WHITMAN

NATIONAL ARCHIVES

First Lt. Ed Flash, leader of F Company's second platoon, was close friends with Calhoun, and together the two men worked to procure items for the 503rd that the army failed to deliver.

Col. George Jones was a West Pointer and an early graduate of the parachute school at Fort Benning, Georgia. As the commander of the 503rd, Jones made the jump over Corregidor alongside his men in the first wave.

NATIONAL ARCHIVES

NATIONAL ARCHIVES

Before the 503rd was ordered to the Pacific, the men of B Company were sent to Salt Lake City, Utah. Soon photographs appeared in American newspapers showing the paratroopers training on skis and jumping in snowsuits. Yet the training was a deception, designed to trick Hitler into assuming the regiment was headed for Norway to fight the Germans. In truth, the unit was bound for Australia.

The 503rd's first combat jump was over Nadzab, New Guinea, in September 1943. The operation was executed perfectly, but for one hitch: the Japanese had left the area. This paratrooper is seen on guard duty at the Nadzab airstrip, armed with a Thompson submachine gun.

NATIONAL ARCHIVES

NATIONAL ARCHIVES

Gen. Douglas MacArthur knew what the men of the 503rd were capable of and insisted on observing their drop on Nadzab for himself. He is seen here with a group of 503rd officers shortly before the regiment departed for the mission.

NATIONAL ARCHIVES

In July 1944, the 503rd was dropped onto the island of Noemfoor, off the northern coast of New Guinea, to help eliminate a Japanese garrison.

NATIONAL ARCHIVES

Gen. Walter Krueger *(left)*, seen here with MacArthur while in New Guinea, was the Sixth Army commander who ordered Col. Jones to take Corregidor.

NATIONAL ARCHIVES

On the island of Mindoro, inside a "war" tent under tight security, Col. Jones uses a model of Corregidor to brief his staff on Rock Force's upcoming mission. By the time he finished, the tropical sun had turned the space into an oven, but the paratroopers' morale had soared.

A little more than four miles in length, Corregidor is shaped like a rocky tadpole facing the mouth of Manila Bay. The "head" of the tadpole is called Topside, where the parachute drops were to be made. Near the base of the "tail" is Malinta Hill.

NATIONAL ARCHIVES

NATIONAL ARCHIVES

Trucks haul paratroopers from the 503rd to the airfield on Mindoro.

NATIONAL ARCHIVES

A row of equipment-laden paratroopers pass the time aboard a C-47 on the way to Corregidor.

NATIONAL ARCHIVES

A view of Corregidor's Topside during the first wave. The white specks are discarded parachutes. Mile Long Barracks can be seen in the upper-left corner.

NATIONAL ARCHIVES

A paratrooper seen just out of the door of his C-47, an instant before the plane's static line deploys his chute. For the assault on Corregidor, the 503rd jumped at only four hundred feet, allowing them mere seconds in the air before they hit the ground.

NATIONAL ARCHIVES

A paratrooper braces for impact before hitting the island's rocky, pockmarked soil. This man was fortunate not to land in a ravine, where soldiers whose parachutes became tangled in trees were easy targets for the Japanese defenders.

NATIONAL ARCHIVES

Pvt. Chet Nycum, the lead scout in G Company, lands hard in a bomb crater.

NATIONAL ARCHIVES

Paratroopers from the second wave arrive over Corregidor. The jagged tree trunks, blasted into sharp daggers by a preinvasion barrage from bombers and US Navy destroyers, represented a real danger to the descending paratroopers.

NATIONAL ARCHIVES

Topside's Mile Long Barracks, the world's longest military barracks, had, prior to the war, been used for the billeting of American officers and enlisted personnel assigned to Fort Mills. During the American invasion to retake the island, the paratroopers seized the barracks from the Japanese who used it as a command post and aid station. Behind the building can be seen the Bataan Peninsula and Mt. Mariveles.

NATIONAL ARCHIVES

Under Japanese fire, Tech. Sgt. Frank Arrigo and Pfc. Clyde Bates scale the pole and raise the American flag over Topside.

NATIONAL ARCHIVES

A cargo plane drops supplies and mail as it passes over the old golf course. The terrain below is riddled with bomb craters, and the rooftops of the former officers' quarters have been demolished.

COURTESY OF PAUL WHITMAN

Calhoun and his first platoon pose with
a captured Japanese machine gun
near Battery Hearn.

NATIONAL ARCHIVES

The Corregidor lighthouse, which sat east of the parade ground overlooking
the golf course, became a headquarters for Bill Calhoun and his men
between patrols.

NATIONAL ARCHIVES

A pack howitzer fires on Topside as paratroopers take cover from enemy counterfire. Mile Long Barracks, where Capt. Bradford had set up an aid station, is in the background.

NATIONAL ARCHIVES

Paratroopers from F Company approach the ordnance machine shop shortly after Pfc. Fred Morgan was killed in a Japanese ambush there. Soon, a 75mm pack howitzer would arrive to assist in the attack on the enemy garrison inside.

NATIONAL ARCHIVES

NATIONAL ARCHIVES

One of the most deadly tasks during the battle was clearing the island's countless caves of enemy defenders. Paratroopers, approaching in groups, would use phosphorus grenades to smoke out the Japanese.

Men line up outside the aid station in Mile Long Barracks.

NATIONAL ARCHIVES

NATIONAL ARCHIVES

Gen. MacArthur and members of his entourage tour a newly liberated Corregidor. When he stepped off the boat at North Dock, the stench of enemy corpses still hung in the air.

NATIONAL ARCHIVES

Paratroopers guard the road to Topside during
Gen. MacArthur's tour of Corregidor.

NATIONAL ARCHIVES

NATIONAL ARCHIVES

Once a resident of Corregidor,
MacArthur found the island
dramatically altered by aerial
bombardment and weeks of intense
fighting. "Gentlemen," the general said
to his staff officers as he surveyed the
damage, "Corregidor is living proof that
the day of the fixed fortress is over."

A group of battle-weary paratroopers rest
in April 1945, likely on Negros Island.

There would be no more snipers harassing 28-D. Calhoun applauded Gifford from afar. It was a bold attack that worked because of decisive action. But it didn't come without a cost. F and D company suffered six killed and fourteen wounded.

With the battery in American hands, Calhoun and his platoon dug in. The sun was setting and they were ordered to remain overnight at Battery Boston. By five P.M., they had a 360-degree perimeter watching a draw at the head of Crockett Ravine. Their western flank was thirty yards from the road to Battery Wheeler. The north side ran along the trail that descended into the ravine. The south side was a sheer cliff. Only the east side worried Calhoun. It was level ground that dropped down into the ravine. He placed his machine gun there.

Before dark, each man got three-quarters of a canteen of water. Many of the men were dry or on their last swallow when the water arrived. Sitting in his foxhole, Calhoun took a few sips. The water tasted amazing. Kipling's line from the poem "Gunga Din" came to mind:

> *But when it comes to slaughter*
> *You will do your work on water,*
> *An' you'll lick the bloomin' boots of 'im that's got it.*

Dark came quickly and soon all Calhoun and his men could see was black. They knew generally where friendly forces were set up, but they also knew Japanese marines were nearby. The wind kicked up and Calhoun heard tin rattling around him.

Then a burst from an American machine gun.

More tin rattling.

Were Japanese marines moving on his position?

The paratroopers were spooked. He could hear his men speaking in hushed tones as they desperately searched for a target. A burst of fire or a grenade exploded after each rattle.

At sea, destroyers patrolling the island sent up illumination shells or star shells. The rounds exploded in a starburst, shining light over the area for a few minutes before burning out. After each shell, Calhoun popped out of his hole and checked the area for bodies or any sign of Japanese trying to infiltrate the perimeter.

He found nothing.

During one illumination period, Calhoun was moving along the line when he spotted some corrugated sheet metal scattered near their position. The sheets were probably damaged from the preinvasion bombardments. He was just about to return to his foxhole when a wind gust rattled the metal. That was his Japanese infiltrators. He passed word to his men and the firing stopped.

Back in his foxhole near Battery Boston, Calhoun smelled smoke in the direction of Battery Wheeler. Ever since Gifford's platoon had saturated the battery with phosphorus grenades, dark smoke streamed out of the doors of the powder magazine. Just before midnight, Calhoun felt the ground shake. It wasn't like the thumping of artillery shells or even an earthquake. It was more like an explosion deep under the ground, as if the island itself were burping. He heard a sucking sound, like someone taking a deep breath through puckered lips, coming from a nearby grate.

Calhoun looked toward Battery Wheeler.

A wall of fire hundreds of feet high roared out of the gunport openings like a volcano. Flames howled into the sky for the next fifteen minutes. The whole battery lit up like it was under the midday sun. A heat wave washed over Calhoun's platoon, forcing them to abandon their position and pull back forty yards. The paratroopers watched the flames flare and then fade. Calhoun tried to make out where Gifford and his men fled, but he didn't see them. It was too dangerous to move at night because the paratroopers were trained to shoot first when they saw movement in the darkness. He ordered his men to dig in again. There was nothing to do until morning.

It was well after midnight when Calhoun finally lay down in his foxhole to rest. He had slept little since his last night on Mindoro and was dead tired. He allowed himself to close his eyes for just a moment. When he opened them again, the sun was shining. For a second, he thought he was back on Mindoro and it was Christmas morning. He half expected to smell roast turkey and see the smiling face of the Australian bulldozer driver again.

Then reality caught up with the sun. He was on Corregidor. He took comfort in surviving another day.

From his position, the area around Battery Boston looked desolate and ravaged in the bright, clear, early morning sunlight. It reminded Calhoun of the pictures of World War I battlefields he had seen in history books. Smoke still rose from the Battery Wheeler magazines, and the odor of burned flesh wafted in the breeze. After some water and a quick breakfast of dried biscuits, Calhoun got orders to lead his platoon toward the battery to link up with Gifford. He hoped the paratroopers had cleared out before the fire, but he wasn't sure.

They cautiously worked their way toward the battery. Calhoun felt the heat emanating from the structure with every step. When they got to the outskirts, Calhoun heard a popping sound, like frying meat. Bodies were burning inside, he thought. Calhoun's men counted forty dead Japanese on their approach. Some had been killed in the fighting the day before. Some by machine-gun fire from Calhoun's section, and some by a .50-caliber machine-gun section on Topside that fired all night.

Calhoun found Gifford and his men back at the battery.

"What happened?" Calhoun said.

Gifford was in the parapet when the flames erupted from the gunports.

"Forty Japs ran out of the battery just before the flames erupted," he said. "We followed."

Gifford realized the battery might explode and started climbing down the steep cliff. Paratroopers and Japanese defenders raced shoulder to shoulder toward the cliffs as flames nipped at their heels.

Pfc. Thomas T. DeLane was killed by the fire. Another paratrooper broke his leg and was dragged along by his buddies toward the parapet and sea cliff. The Japanese and Americans both hung on bushes and traded blows or slashes with bayonets and trench knives as they climbed down the cliff.

As the fire raged, the Americans clung to the brush on the cliff. They didn't want to stray too far from Topside and the American lines. The Japanese didn't stop and disappeared down below. When the fire died down, the paratroopers climbed back to the top and took up positions near the battery. The next morning, Gifford told Calhoun they found sixty-five Japanese bodies incinerated inside.

The great battery, which stood impenetrable the day before, was now a tomb.

CHAPTER 11

Gold Stars

BEING THAT BRADFORD spent much of the battle in or near the aid station, he picked up stories from all over the battlefield, which he recorded in a journal that later turned into an unpublished manuscript that was passed around by veterans of the battle.

One story was of Pfc. Frank Keller's jump and first two nights on Corregidor. Keller, a member of D Company, landed short in Crockett Ravine. He was supposed to land on B landing field—the golf course—but Keller left the plane too early and came up short, crashing into the brush and landing in the trees in the deep ravine.

Keller struggled to get loose, finally opening his reserve chute and using the static line to climb down. It was about a forty-foot drop and he burned his hands on the line as he slid to the ground.

C-47s thundered overhead and American and Japanese

machine-gun fire cut through the aircraft noise as Keller picked his way through the brush toward Topside. The Japanese held Corregidor's five ravines—Government, Crockett, Cheney, James, and Engineer. The ravines were not named on the maps issued to the paratroopers, though the maps did show fifty-foot contours. Until a ravine's name could be established, they tended to be considered by the army slang term "Indian Country."

Keller had fallen into Indian Country.

The paratroopers not injured by the tangle of trees and brush in the ravine were forced to fight their way back to Topside and American lines. Keller was following an overgrown trail when he ran across a group of paratroopers huddled near some trees. Pfc. Calvin Martin was sitting at the base of a tree with a broken ankle.

Keller fell in with the group as they were discussing what to do with Martin.

"Leave me," Martin told First Lt. Charles Preston, his platoon leader. "This is one hell of a place to break a leg, Lieutenant, but I guess I've done it. I'll hide out down here, but when there's time will you send some men back to get me?"

Preston didn't want to leave. A wounded man was a dead man if the Japanese caught him. But Preston also knew they couldn't stay with him. He and the rest of the paratroopers had to rally with their company.

"Take these extra clips of ammo in case you need 'em," Preston said. "We'll send a platoon down by nightfall."

The paratroopers were about to leave when Keller spoke up.

"I'm just a rifleman, Lieutenant," he said. "They can spare me from my squad, so let me stay with Martin here. I can help him if things get tough."

Preston looked relieved. He agreed to leave Keller and promised to send some men back for them as soon as possible. As Preston led the small group of paratroopers who drifted off course toward Topside, Keller helped Martin into a nearby bomb crater. The pair stayed low and waited in silence, for fear that even a whisper would give away their location.

Soon, the paratroopers heard Japanese coming up the ravine. They crashed through the brush as they worked their way toward Topside and the growing number of paratroopers. A few passed so close to the crater, Keller and Martin heard them talking.

Keller slowly raised his head above the lip of the crater. Three Japanese soldiers were crawling in the underbrush nearby. He started to raise his rifle, but one shot would give away their position. The only thing they could do was hide. He slid back down to the bottom and waited, never taking his eye off the edge of the hole.

Outside the crater, the Japanese voices grew louder. One soldier got within fifteen yards of their hideout. Both paratroopers held their breath. Keller gripped his rifle ready to fire, but no target materialized. Soon, the voices faded into the cacophony of aircraft engines and machine-gun fire.

With the Japanese coming up the ravine, Keller had an idea.

"Let's crawl down toward the sea," Keller said. "I'm afraid those Nips will come back before dark."

The roar of battle covered their movements as they crawled

toward the sea. When they found a hole with a tree over the top of it, Keller signaled to Martin to get inside. Keller crawled forward to scout out the area. He came up over the rise and saw the back of a Japanese defender's head. The man was close enough to touch. He ducked back down behind the berm and moved to a better vantage point in a nearby crater.

Popping back up, he spotted a sack of rice and gas masks. Farther down the ravine was a rally point for the Japanese defenders. Keller crawled out of the hole slowly and made his way back toward Martin's hiding place.

Keller rolled into the crater next to Martin, squeezing together under the tree trunk. All around them they heard Japanese voices. Keller figured a squad at least was coming back to their bivouac for the night. They were stuck. Any movement would give them away. It was getting dark and they didn't want to be caught in the open. They had no choice but to hide out and wait for daylight to move back up the hill.

They both lay awake as the sun faded into darkness. The pain kept Martin up. His broken ankle throbbed. But as the night wore on, Keller had to fight off sleep. All of the adrenaline of the jump and then dodging Japanese soldiers faded into exhaustion. Each time his head dropped and he dozed, Martin poked him hard in the back.

Then, both men heard snoring. One of the Japanese soldiers was sleeping nearby. The snoring became the soundtrack of the night. His snores cascaded into the hole, providing some rare comfort. As long as the paratroopers heard the snores they knew where the Japanese were located.

At dawn, the snoring was replaced by the barking of orders. Keller heard the soldiers stir and start to prepare for the day's fighting. There was chatter. The scraping of equipment being put on or picked up.

Keller heard the crunching of dirt and brush grow louder. A soldier came into view. He was walking near the lip of the hole. He took a step and his boot caught a branch. He stumbled, almost falling into the hole. Keller readied his rifle. At the last second, the soldier regained his balance. He paused for a second and then moved on, unaware that Keller and Martin were under the tree.

Both men finally exhaled.

As the sun rose higher into the sky, the two paratroopers heard heavy fighting above them. They knew each shot meant the chance of a rescue was slim. There was no way Preston was coming as long as the ravine was contested.

Martin urged Keller to leave him.

"You better get out of here," he said. "I'll be all right if I lay low, and you could make it down to the beach, where some boat might pick you up."

Keller refused.

"I'm going to find a path to the beach," he said, crawling out of the hole. He searched for a path, keeping his head down and moving slowly. Most of the Japanese were above him, and the intermittent fire covered his movement. The ravine was steep and rocky. Impossible for Martin and his broken ankle to negotiate.

Back in the hole, Keller told Martin the bad news. They were stuck. With nothing to do but wait, they broke out some rations and shared a meal of dry biscuits and some canned eggs-and-ham. They exchanged sips from a canteen of water. Their last one was held in reserve.

Up on Topside, Preston never stopped thinking of Keller and Martin. He tried to get a rescue party the first day, but he and his men were needed in the perimeter. Preston planned to head down and get Keller and Martin the morning of the second day, but he was sent out on patrols. Finally, at the end of the second day, Preston got approval to take three squads down Crockett Ravine to find Keller and Martin.

Back at the hole, the fighting had moved to the west and for the first time Keller and Martin let themselves think about a rescue.

"Guess they'll come down for us tomorrow," Keller told Martin, trying to keep his injured comrade's spirits up.

That night, all Preston could think about were Martin and Keller. Down in Crockett Ravine, Keller and Martin had another sleepless night.

Out of water and hungry, Keller and Martin heard a group of soldiers approaching at dawn. Keller took a grenade off his belt and loosened the pin so he could throw it quickly. Each crunch of dirt or the snap of a stick was terror. Keller didn't dare poke his head out for fear of attracting attention. Both paratroopers were sure it was the Japanese squad coming back. Keller's eyes darted back and forth as he waited for a head to appear at the edge of the crater as he cradled the grenade.

Then he heard talking. English. Keller and Martin exhaled, relieved.

But not as much as Preston.

"Thank God you're all right," said Preston when he discovered the paratroopers in the bottom of the hole. "I kept thinking the Japs would capture you."

"They might have," Keller said, fixing the grenade pin, "but they'd been dead."

Back at the aid station, Bradford was impressed by the story as he treated Martin's leg. There was something about the tale that resonated with him. It wasn't just the courage to face the Japanese alone or the cunning to hide out among them.

It was the selflessness of Keller's action.

Without thinking about his own safety, Keller had stayed with Martin and never considered abandoning him. They were a team, keeping each other awake throughout two long and dangerous nights. It was the epitome of the brotherhood of the 503rd. In Bradford's eyes, men like Keller and Martin represented the best of the regiment.

"Such men do not need to die to win gold stars," Bradford wrote about Keller and Martin. "They are born with them."

CHAPTER 12

Dug In

THE AREA AROUND Battery Wheeler was calm.

The machine guns in Crockett Ravine were quiet. No bullets cracked overhead, rattling the paratroopers' eardrums. All around Calhoun, his men picked up souvenirs off the Japanese dead. Uniform insignia. *Shin guntō* swords from the officers, which were both a weapon and a symbol of rank. Pistols. Calhoun passed some of the mortar platoon posing for a picture in front of an old M3 antiaircraft gun left there from when the Americans held the island.

But Calhoun ignored the detritus of war. The silence ate at him. The lull let his mind wander. *The Japanese defenders must all be dead,* Calhoun thought. The battle was over, he hoped. He wanted to believe that, but in his guts, he knew it wasn't true. They'd been fighting for two days now and he was tired.

Dirty.

Hot.

But most of all, thirsty. Each man jumped with two full canteens, but after a day and a half of fighting that water was almost gone. As Calhoun's platoon left Battery Wheeler and patrolled back to 28-D, he could think only about water. To his surprise, when the platoon got back to Topside they were greeted with a canteen of water and three K-rations in tan rectangular cardstock boxes. U.S. ARMY FIELD RATION K was printed on the top of each box with the meal type—breakfast, supper, dinner—printed underneath.

After all his men took some food and water, Calhoun unscrewed the top of a canteen and took a swig. The water was lukewarm, but it tasted glorious. The best water he'd ever had. He took another swig and sat down to a meal. All around him, his men dug into the K-rations. The paratroopers ate the food with little excitement. K-rations were made up of mostly canned meat and eggs, tasteless biscuits, and processed cheese. Meals also came with gum or candy and cigarettes.

Calhoun and the others sat on the ground. Their faces were gaunt and sallow. Their skin was yellow from atabrine, a bitter yellow pill given to soldiers in the Pacific to fend off malaria. After filling their bellies, the paratroopers filled their bandoliers with ammunition.

While Calhoun and his platoon had been away at Battery Boston, Bailey had sent the rest of the company back to Topside's ammo dump. They brought back mortar rounds, extra bandoliers of ammunition for the riflemen, and as many fragmentation and white phosphorus hand grenades as they could carry. The supply of ammo was plentiful. The riflemen filled the pouches on their rifle belts and some picked up an extra bandolier of eight M1 clips just in case.

All morning, as F Company ate, drank, and smoked, not a single shot.

Life was improving.

Until Bailey pulled Calhoun into 28-D to talk about a new mission. The officers stood over a poorly drawn map.

"I need your guys to capture this battery here," Bailey said, pointing to a pair of guns on the western side of the island.

Originally called Battery Smith One and Battery Smith Two, prewar Coast Artillery, Corregidor soldiers called the batteries Pat and Pending, after a popular radio commercial of the era. Located north of Battery Wheeler, and one thousand feet apart, the batteries were eventually broken up. Battery One kept the Smith name. The second battery's name was changed to Hearn. The pair of guns were formidable. Unlike the guns in Battery Wheeler, Smith and Hearn weren't enclosed in a concrete bowl, so they could elevate higher, thereby improving their range. They could fire shells almost twenty miles out to sea. Any enemy ships attempting to navigate into Manila Bay would come under fire from Batteries Smith and Hearn first. The guns had been sabotaged by Americans preparing to surrender in 1942. By 1945, the guns were still out of commission, but the Japanese were likely living in the battery's storage spaces.

Calhoun looked at the map. He spotted some trolley tracks that took him to Battery Hearn. From there, he'd turn west and follow the ridge to the objective.

"Who are the nearest friendlies?" he said.

Bailey told him the rest of F Company was on Topside.

"We'll be about seven hundred yards away," Bailey said.

That was no comfort to Calhoun. Once at Battery Smith, he had no way of contacting the company at night when the radio net was deactivated. That far out, he was on his own. But he had no choice. It was the only way to clear the batteries and secure Topside.

An hour later, the first platoon paratroopers, with McCarter in the lead and Pfc. John Bartlett, the second scout, right behind him, left 28-D heading toward the head of the tadpole-shaped island. McCarter and Bartlett led the platoon around the bombed-out remnants of the storage and maintenance garages without incident and then started down the trolley bed.

The trolley cars had once hauled passengers, ammunition, and supplies on the narrow-gauge railroad around the island fortress before the Japanese took Corregidor. But now, the tracks were long gone and the whole area was overgrown. Calhoun kept his eyes on the woods, searching for any sign of trouble. Most of the area had escaped bombardment, so the trees were thick with tangled vines and a canopy that kept out the afternoon sun.

When McCarter spotted suspicious areas, he sprayed them with bursts from his Thompson submachine gun.

Soon they were out of the cover of trees and vegetation and in a deep railroad cut with steep concrete walls. Once they were in the cut, there was no way to climb out. The platoon moved quickly, not wanting to get trapped. They found a break along the east wall and escaped before the Japanese discovered them.

When they got back to level ground, Calhoun could see the bare, bomb-scarred hill of Battery Hearn, Smith's twin. No foliage was left around the battery. The area was completely pockmarked with craters. Shattered trees poked out of the ground. The limbs were mangled. The few still standing reached up into the sky as if they were begging for salvation. The paratroopers kicked up dust as they crossed the scarred ground toward a round concrete pad where the twelve-inch barbette-mounted gun stood. The gun sat in the middle of concrete rings, which resembled a bull's-eye. A giant barrel from the sabotaged gun was lying at the base of the magazine. Calhoun had seen a photograph of this battery before, only it was a Japanese photograph of a group of soldiers celebrating their triumph over Corregidor in 1942.

A hill sat behind the gun. It must be the magazine, Calhoun thought as they approached. Each gun had a concrete magazine buried under a hill of dirt. The manmade hill was steep on three sides, but the east side sloped back toward the road.

Near the magazine's entrance were ashes from campfires. Calhoun stopped at the mouth of the magazine and peered inside. He saw Japanese rations stacked to the ceiling. Iron rings were embedded in the walls of the tunnel. Steel frames, which folded against the wall, hung from the rings. The frames held mattresses where the prewar American gun crew slept when they were on alert. Now the tunnels were manned by Japanese defenders who slept and ate in the shelters.

After passing Hearn, the platoon advanced down the ridge toward Battery Smith in echelon formation, or in a diagonal line. The formation gave each man a clear view of what lay ahead and the paratroopers had overlapping fields of fire. As the platoon approached the northwest side of Smith magazine, Pfc. Richard Aimers from Tennessee called out to Pvt. Bill McDonald.

"Look up on that hill," he said. "There's a Jap observer standing out in the open and he's looking at us through his binoculars."

A Japanese officer's head was peeking slightly above a berm by the battery. He was watching the paratroopers advance.

"Don't worry about him," McDonald said. "We'll take care of him in a few minutes when we get up there."

Aimers shouldered his M1 Garand. No one believed Aimers was that good a shot, despite his last name.

"You'll never in a million years be able to hit him from this range," McDonald said.

Aimers fired one shot.

McDonald was watching the Japanese officer and saw his head snap back and the binoculars fall as his body disappeared behind the berm. Aimers lowered his Garand as Bartlett, the scout, came running over.

"I just saw a Jap down there, and I shot him, and I want those binoculars when we get there," Aimers told Bartlett, knowing he'd be in the lead since he was a scout.

The platoon kept advancing, this time cautiously since they weren't sure if more Japanese were in the area. Japanese officers didn't travel alone. When they reached the battery, the paratroopers fanned out. Battery Smith looked like Battery Hearn, with the same large hill with a magazine buried underneath it. Bartlett and McCarter approached the door with their weapons at the ready. Bartlett spotted some cement steps that led down to the fire direction center, the area where the gun, when in operation, was aimed and fired. There is usually one fire direction center for six guns.

The steel door was closed. When Bartlett opened it, a rifle shot rang out. The paratroopers called for the Japanese to come out and surrender. When that failed, Bartlett alerted Calhoun, who called over the flamethrower team.

Bartlett waited for the signal from the flamethrower operator and then opened the door wide. The flamethrower operator sent a stream of fire into the opening. Flames engulfed the threshold of the door and the tunnel inside. Thick smoke flooded from the concrete room.

Calhoun and Bartlett peered into the room as the magazines burned. In the smoke and darkness, they spotted movement. They raised their rifles as, like shot from a cannon, several Japanese marines burst out the door and up the stairs, their hair and uniforms aflame. The paratroopers opened fire. The Japanese dropped, struck down by a cascade of bullets.

Calhoun sent his first squad inside the tunnel after the flames subsided. They found whiskey, San Miguel beer, and a five-gallon jug of sake. Calhoun knew the Japanese were likely hiding in there, but he didn't have the manpower to clear out the long tunnel. He set a guard on the door and climbed to the top of the magazine to work on a defensive plan for the night.

Nearby, Aimers was on top of the battery with McDonald, searching for the body of the officer he'd shot. He found it crumpled on the ground facedown. The back of his skull was smashed. When Aimers rolled the body over, he found the binoculars. The bullet had sliced through the left eyepiece and hit the officer in the face. It was a one-in-a-million shot. The field glasses were ruined. Aimers's excellent marksmanship robbed him of a fine pair of binoculars, but he stuffed them into a cargo pocket as a souvenir anyway.

From the top of the magazine, Calhoun took stock of his position. He was still uneasy with the isolation of his platoon. After the fight in the tunnel, he had the ominous feeling that there was a large Japanese force nearby, very likely watching them. And his position was too near the sea, out of sight of the other forces.

The magazine hill could easily be defended because of its steep sides, but there was nowhere to go if he was attacked. It was too much like the Alamo, whose history Calhoun, a Texan, knew too well.

Calhoun checked his watch. It was late afternoon. If his men were going to have a chance, he wanted to get dug in before dark. As he set his men into a defensive position, a Japanese machine gun opened up. The rounds exploded nearby or cracked overhead.

"Find some cover!" Calhoun yelled at his men.

Calhoun found a nearby crater and scanned the brush, searching for the machine gunner after he fired another burst. Instead of ducking his head, Calhoun kept watch. He noticed each burst shook a wood-covered knoll about a hundred yards west of the battery.

Pvt. Benedict Schilli, the third squad BAR gunner, got into a prone position on the concrete pad near the gun. Shouldering the rifle, he squeezed off a burst. The rounds sliced through the trees. He fired again, each burst creeping closer to the knoll where the machine gunner was attacking. Once Schilli got in range, he poured several bursts into the knoll. There was no more machine-gun fire after that. Two days later, on patrol, the platoon found the abandoned machine gun. A camouflage net laced with vegetation hung in front of the gun. Stakes kept the net in place. Calhoun knelt next to the gun. One of Schilli's rounds had hit the gun's receiver, disabling it. Nearby, he spotted dried blood on the leaves.

With the machine gun out of commission, a quiet settled over the area. Calhoun was preparing to send in a squad to clear the magazine tunnel when a runner arrived, sent by First Lt. Bailey with new orders. He wanted Calhoun to pull back up the ridge, set up near Battery Hearn, and link up with some reinforcements. The new position was closer to Bailey's position on Way Hill, and he could cover Grubbs Road, a direct approach to Topside. An enemy attack toward Topside would likely use the road. Calhoun checked his watch—it was nearly five P.M. They'd have to hurry to make it to the new position and dig in before dark.

"OK," he told his men. "We're moving back to the other battery. Police up your area. We leave in five minutes."

The paratroopers gathered their equipment and fell into line.

Calhoun led them across the concrete pad west toward Battery Hearn. They moved quickly back up the hill and arrived at the battery at the same time as reinforcements sent by Bailey. Two rifle squads from the second platoon, two squads from the mortar platoon, a light machine-gun section from the battalion Headquarters Company, and a bazooka team.

First Lt. Dan Lee, a new officer in the company, led the reinforcements over from Way Hill. Second Lt. John Mara, on loan for the night from the battalion headquarters, was sent along to help out too.

When Calhoun got to Battery Hearn, he went right to the top of the magazine. The hill offered a formidable position. It was rectangular in shape, about eighty yards long and forty yards across. The north, south, and west sides were so steep they could be climbed only with great difficulty. The east side sloped gradually down to a railway cut a hundred yards behind the magazine.

Directly opposite from the center of the magazine in a ravine were the remnants of two destroyed trolley cars, overturned on their sides. Calhoun could see the cars' floors from his position on top of the battery.

South of the hill, clumps of trees concealed Belt Line Road as it skirted the upper reaches of Cheney Ravine. The heavier forest started after Belt Line Road. In the late afternoon, it appeared dark and sinister.

A deep gully separated him from the rest of the company headquarters on Way Hill. Bailey had third platoon, one squad from second platoon, a 60mm mortar squad, and a section of light machine guns from battalion. He couldn't see Bailey's position because Way Hill was still heavily wooded, but at least at Battery Hearn he was closer to Bailey and support from Topside.

From his vantage point, Calhoun figured the biggest danger was from the east side. It was a gradual slope leading to the road. Darkness was rapidly approaching. Realizing it would be night before he could supervise every detail of the defense, Calhoun called Second Lt. Mara over.

"Get this gun emplaced," he told him, showing Mara how he wanted the machine gun oriented.

Calhoun had twenty-four riflemen, including three BARs, defending about forty yards. He called over first squad to cover the road since it was the enemy's most probable line of approach. The second squad set up on the north side. And his third squad covered the west and south sides. Staff Sgt. John Phillips, F Company's mortar platoon sergeant, put his two mortars at opposite ends of the perimeter. Nicknamed "Red Horse," Phillips was a former Hollywood stuntman. Both mortars were zeroed in on where the railroad crossed Grubbs Road.

While the paratroopers dug in, a pair of mortar shells sailed out of the sky and exploded, sending shrapnel in all directions. No one was hurt, but the attack got Phillips's attention. He popped his head up and looked toward the railcars. The shells had come from that direction. He alerted his own mortar crews and the paratroopers manned their guns.

"Five rounds, let's go," Phillips said.

The loader snatched a shell from the pile with both hands and held it over the barrel of the mortar waiting for Phillips's order.

"Hang it. Fire! Hang it. Fire!"

Thump. Thump. Thump. The shells were dropped in succession. They arced up and slammed into the brush near the railroad cars. After the explosions, nothing stirred and there was no return fire. The crews stood down and everybody went back to preparing their fighting position for the night.

With everything in place, Calhoun selected a crater next to the magazine's ventilator shaft near the top of the hill as his command post. The shaft was topped at the surface by a concrete housing with large openings on each side. Inside the shaft, steel rungs were set in the concrete to form a ladder to the floor of the magazine. The shaft gave an intrepid enemy an opportunity to scale the ladder and hurl out a grenade or spray the Americans with gunfire. Calhoun didn't have time to clear out the magazine below. Instead, he pulled his runners, Mikel and Thompson, aside.

"Watch the shafts," he said. "Make sure no Jap crawls up."

As the last rays of light disappeared into the South China Sea, Calhoun shut off his radio and the paratroopers hunkered down in their positions. It was standard operating procedure in the jungle to silence the radio for fear that its random squawking might give away their location. For the rest of the night, Calhoun's platoon was isolated on top of the magazine. He sat in the crater near the ventilation shaft and waited. Even though he was in a better position, Calhoun still couldn't shake the feeling that the Japanese defenders were nearby.

It was shaping up to be a long night.

———

DOWN IN CHENEY RAVINE, Imperial Navy Lieutenant Takeji Endo prepared for an attack. For two days, he'd been trying to hold the line as the American paratroopers slowly advanced from Topside and the Thirty-Fourth Infantry soldiers rooted out his defenders on Malinta Hill. Endo had taken command of the island's defense after Capt. Akira Itagaki was killed on the day of the parachute assault. Itagaki had been surveying the battlefield when some paratroopers who missed the landing field were working their way up to Topside. They spotted the captain outside of his bunker and opened fire, killing him, according to Itagaki's captured Korean orderly.

The parachute assault caught Itagaki off guard.

The defensive plan was for Japanese Army troops and provisional naval formations, made up of sailors from the ships sunk in Philippine waters, to man fixed defensive positions guarding the landing beaches. Poorly trained and equipped, some of the provisional units had one rifle for five men. The rest were armed with metal poles tipped with bayonets, which Calhoun and the paratroopers witnessed on the first night. Once the amphibious attack stalled, the Japanese marines would counterattack and sweep the Americans from the beach.

With all of their defenses aimed at the sea, they had little chance of stopping the paratroopers, who now held the high ground. Endo knew he had to take back the strategic advantage because his men needed water, food, and ammunition.

Endo had three battalions of Japanese marines in bombproof concrete shelters at the bottom of Grubbs Ravine. His plan was to dislodge the paratroopers from Topside at night from the western end of the island with two columns.

Column A would climb Grubbs Ravine and attack American positions at Battery Hearn. Endo would lead Column B up Cheney Ravine and attack from the west to seize Topside from that direction. Column A would attack around midnight. Column B would attack an hour later, taking advantage of the confusion and chaos caused by the initial attack. Endo assured his officers the attack would work. The plan was toasted with a bottle of sake and salutes to the emperor and their homeland. The officers chanted between shots: "May the emperor live ten thousand years."

CHAPTER 13

Blood for the Emperor

A STAR SHELL from one of the destroyers patrolling the black seas around the island shot into the sky. Riding a trail of smoke, it hit the top of its trajectory and exploded, lighting up the area around Battery Hearn.

Calhoun popped his head up above the lip of the crater and scanned the rubble and brush down in the road for any sign of the Japanese. He squinted, looking for any movement as the shell slowly burned out and night overtook the light once again.

Calhoun rolled back into the crater with his two runners and waited for the next shell. There was no pattern to the firing. No schedule. The shells seemed to appear at random like lightning bugs. One second light. The next second dark. So far, he hadn't needed light. Everything was quiet since the two mortar rounds had struck the top of the hill just after sunset.

Exhausted and thirsty, Calhoun lay down on the edge of the crater next to the large ventilator shaft. The concrete roof from the shaft extended overhead about a foot, giving him some cover. It was around midnight and Calhoun finally let his eyes close, when he heard loud yelling along the eastern perimeter.

Endo's A Column was coming up Grubbs Ravine.

Calhoun grabbed his helmet and rifle and crawled to the edge of the hill. The shouting was coming from the railroad cut. It started with a single voice. Then a group chanted a reply. Call and response. Call and response. The volume increased as the group got closer. Soon, the response came right on top of the call until it blended into a climax.

All around him the paratroopers on the eastern side of the hill stirred. Those asleep were shaken awake. Men shouldered their rifles. The machine-gun crews made sure extra belts of ammunition were ready. They knew what was coming.

Banzai.

The paratroopers had heard stories about the Japanese tactic. They'd heard the stories of Bloody Ridge on Guadalcanal. The Japanese charging and screaming "Banzai!" "Totsugeki!" (charge), or "Blood for the Emperor!" Some even yelled, "Marine, you die!" Now it was the paratroopers' turn.

The yelling grew closer, the sound rolling up the ravine like a wave. Each response louder than the first.

Call.

Response.

CALL!

RESPONSE!

Calhoun couldn't make out the exact words. As he listened, bits of cement from the overhang stung his face. The chanting was masking the sound of machine-gun rounds from the valley covering the advance. First squad fired back. They didn't see a target, but they weren't going to let a challenge go unanswered.

Then the crackle of a star shell broke through the cacophony of gunfire. Calhoun saw the shell rocket into the sky, then arrows of light cut through the darkness until Grubbs Road was under a spotlight. Calhoun peered down from the hill. There, to his disbelief, were Japanese Imperial Marines marching up Grubbs Road in columns of four.

It looked like a parade, or columns of troops during the Civil War. No one was looking for cover. They were marching in formation up the road, chanting, moving steadily forward. Japanese officers in the rear, their swords out, were goading the men on, leading the chants, making certain that no man lagged behind. Calhoun looked past the first rank. The formation snaked down the road as far as Calhoun could see. They were heading for Topside.

So much for less than 1,000 defenders.

The Japanese would be in range in minutes. Calhoun turned to one of his squad leaders.

"Get a bandolier of ammo from every rifleman over there and BAR clips," Calhoun ordered, sending the paratrooper scrambling over to the southwest side of the hill.

He turned to Thompson.

"Crawl up to Lee and Phillips and check the situation," he said, knowing the mortars were his best weapon to break up the attack.

Mikel was still watching the shafts when Calhoun sent him

to the north side to check on the first squad and the machine guns. Behind him, Calhoun heard the thump of mortars.

"Hang it. Fire!"

The rounds whistled into the air, coming down on the Japanese defenders at the head of the column. Razor-sharp shrapnel cut down the first men in line. They fell to the ground, some dead, others writhing in pain. Those behind stepped over the fallen men, filling the ranks and advancing.

Calhoun heard a steady thump behind him as more mortar rounds arced over his head and crashed down on the Japanese, scattering the ranks for a few seconds before they re-formed, gaps filling in again as the defenders advanced. Calhoun watched some of the Japanese defenders throw up as they staggered past their fallen comrades. The paratroopers had heard that the Japanese soldiers drank beer and liquor before a banzai attack. A little liquid courage before their officers drove them into a certain death.

The mortar rounds took a toll on the ranks, but the Japanese continued to advance, crossing the intersection of Grubbs and Belt Line Road. They were past Battery Hearn and heading for Topside, and there was nothing Calhoun could do. He cursed under his breath. Had he been able to notify higher headquarters over the radio, they could have called in naval fire from the cruisers and destroyers lying offshore, or called in the 75mm howitzers or 81mm mortars on Topside and snuffed out the attack.

Instead, all the navy could do was shoot star shells.

Phillips, in one of the mortar pits in the middle of the perimeter, did his best to beat the Japanese back. His crews kept up a steady barrage of mortar rounds at first, but Calhoun heard the thump of the mortar slow. Each gun had about fifty rounds. By now the supply was exhausted, and the Japanese were still coming.

As soon as they were in range, the American .30-caliber machine guns opened up, knocking down the front ranks and slicing through the column. The holes filled up as if with water, and the Japanese soldiers pressed forward. Staff Sgt. Donald White, a squad leader in second platoon, was dug in on the east side. As the Japanese pressed on, he moved out to protect his squad's flank, and was hit by a machine-gun burst.

He died instantly.

As the thinning column neared the overturned trolley cars, the Japanese soldiers moved off the road toward the base of Way Hill. First Lt. Bailey was set up on top and his men opened fire, hitting them from the opposite side.

But no amount of gunfire would deter the marines from drawing blood for their emperor. No doubt, in the rear, Japanese officers urged them on by questioning their sense of duty and, when that failed, with the tip of their swords. But to the paratroopers, the Japanese defenders just kept coming.

The battle raged under a parade of star shells. It was like a long blink. One second, the Japanese were illuminated. Easy targets. But then the darkness returned. When it did, Calhoun knew some of the Japanese were slipping past and heading for Topside. When the next shell rose into the sky, the Japanese were gone.

They'd pulled back down the road.

There were Japanese troops in the ravine. A lot of them. He figured they'd found shelter in the tunnels but were now massing for another attack. They'd stopped the first attempt, but they'd be back.

Calhoun took a deep breath and said a quick prayer. He thanked God for watching over him and his men. He also asked that God continue his watch because he was still in harm's way. Then he was up on his feet, moving down the line checking on his men. Ammunition was running low despite the extra supply taken from the ammo dump earlier. He knew if they ran out of ammunition, they'd be overrun.

"Fix bayonets," Calhoun said.

He then told each of the paratroopers that the rest of F Company was about three hundred yards away on top of Way Hill, across Grubbs Road.

"You know where the rest of the company is," he said, in case they were overrun. A survivor would have to get across a column of advancing Japanese marines first, but at least there were friendly faces nearby. "Try to get through and get across there to the company. That's all we can do."

IT WAS JUST after midnight when Lieutenant Endo assembled almost a thousand Japanese marines at the western end of Cheney Trail. Topside was five hundred feet above, and the marines slowly worked their way up the sloping trail under a black, moonless night.

They reached Topside without being detected. The Japanese marines made it within fifty yards of Company D's lines when they stumbled into a squad set up across the trail.

The Japanese startled the paratroopers and the attackers were past the squad before a shot was fired.

The lead marines kept pressing forward when they ran into First Lt. John Lindgren's mortar platoon, set up in a crater in the middle of Cheney Trail. Lindgren's men managed to get off a few 60mm rounds, a gesture more than anything else during a confusing fight where nothing could be seen.

Subdued voices started giving commands, and a few paratroopers shot at movement. In the chaos the survivors fell back to a bunker off the trail. They fired their rifles at the vague shapes of Japanese marines, who were shouting and milling about in confusion in the darkness in front of them.

Once the head of the column stopped, the Japanese bunched up on the narrow trail. Endo pressed the attack instead of bypassing the company.

Unlike Calhoun, D Company was boxed in by steep cliffs. The paratroopers had nowhere to go, and like F Company, they had no way of calling for help.

First Lt. Joseph Turinsky was in the plotting room of Battery Wheeler during the banzai attack. He'd just established his command post after replacing Gifford's platoon. He'd been unable to tie in with Bailey and Calhoun's position on the ravine's north side, leaving a five-hundred-yard gap between the two companies.

The Japanese marines drove Turinsky's men back as they

charged toward Topside. The paratroopers fell back to a crater and bunker near Wheeler Point, a small outcropping southeast of the battery. Lindgren and the surviving paratroopers from the mortar platoon and skirmish line, having abandoned the crater in the middle of the trail, joined Turinsky and his men. A wild shootout erupted at extremely close quarters. With nothing but a sheer drop at their backs, the paratroopers stopped wave after wave of frenzied attacks. Turinsky tried to rally his men by climbing on top of the bunker's blast wall and firing his carbine but was quickly killed by rifle fire.

At Battery Hearn, Calhoun heard the gunfire around Wheeler Point. His men were only a few hundred yards away as the crow flies, but there was nothing he could do. He had his own problems. Between attacks, he worked his way down the line, checking on his men. Jacked on adrenaline, they were finding that the waiting was worse than combat. During the lull, whatever nightmares each paratrooper could conjure came to fruition. Every noise was the enemy. Any second they expected to get overrun.

Finally, after an hour, the chanting started again. Faint at first. Then louder and louder. Soon, Calhoun saw the fuzzy outline of the columns coming back up the road. He looked up into the black sky.

Where are the flares? he thought, trying to will a star shell into the sky to illuminate the area.

When the column was in range, the paratroopers opened fire again. Lampman's BAR was set up on a concrete base. As the battle raged, he was left alone near the top of the magazine. Set to single shot, his BAR got off a few rounds at a time. He never opened up fully automatic. The Japanese likely thought he was just a rifleman and concentrated fire on the machine guns down the line, allowing him to cut down marine after marine.

Private McCarter was in the third squad, positioned on the south side of the hill, facing away from the action. He had heard the first attack, of course, and desperately wanted to get involved when the second one started. Like Calhoun, he had heard the chants start up again. The thump of the mortar, the rattle of the .30-caliber machine guns, rifle fire filling the gaps—his blood was boiling as the east side of the hill erupted. McCarter saw a few Japanese skirt past the hill and head up toward Topside. There was a gap near the northeast corner of the hill. He leveled his Thompson submachine gun to fire, but realized the distance from the hill to the road was too great. He was out of range.

McCarter scanned the area and spotted some high ground near the entrance to a tunnel that led to a storage house for explosives, gas, and powder. McCarter grabbed his Thompson and headed down the hill. He found a spot in a shallow gully near a bump, which was where the trolley tunnel ran into this corner of the hill, supplying the magazine with heavy munitions and equipment. He squatted in the gully and opened fire.

This time the column was in range.

McCarter laid his Thompson over one of his big, heavy arms and pumped short burst after short burst into the Japanese column. He yelled obscenities at the Japanese between shots. What exactly he was calling was lost in the cacophony of battle, but it was obvious to those on the hill, whether in earshot or not, that

McCarter was making his presence known, and not the least concerned with his welfare.

He was one of those rare individuals who was in a state of great exhilaration in combat. Utterly fearless, he didn't seem to consider his own safety there in the gully, alone and exposed. He simply saw the enemy, and attacked. A few Japanese went down, and he shifted the muzzle of his Thompson to the next cluster of men in line and fired. He emptied several magazines into the oncoming banzai charge.

Then click.

He pulled the trigger again but the gun didn't kick. The submachine gun wouldn't fire. It was jammed or broken.

McCarter didn't have time to figure out which. The Japanese were still coming. He scrambled up the hill and saw Schilli's BAR lying in the dirt. Next to the rifle lay Schilli, wounded, having taken shrapnel in the left leg. He was out of the fight. McCarter snatched the rifle and scrounged for more ammo. Racing back to the bump, he got behind the BAR and squeezed off burst after burst, the .30-06 rounds cutting into the columns, knocking Japanese to the dirt. He fed the powerful rifle one magazine after another. There was no shortage of targets as McCarter blazed away.

Then the BAR jammed.

McCarter tried to clear it, but failed. Back up the hill he went, this time returning to the gully with an M1 Garand and a bandolier of ammo. Clip after clip ejected as he poured rounds into the oncoming Japanese attackers. When there were no more

Japanese on the road, he stopped firing and sat back into the hole.

There were over thirty Japanese bodies around the gully.

Soon, rounds cracked over McCarter's head. A Nambu light machine gun was firing at him. McCarter couldn't pinpoint where the Japanese marines were set up. He tried to lure them out by firing at the trolley cars. Finally, he exposed himself so they could see him. When the Japanese opened up again, Mc-Carter ducked down and zeroed in on their position. They were set up near the overturned trolley cars as he had suspected, just north of his position. He fired clip after clip as fast as his finger could squeeze the M1's trigger.

Ping.

The clip ejected and he slid another one home. But the rifle wouldn't fire. McCarter cleared the chamber, but the rifle wasn't jammed. The operating rod was split. The Garand's operating rods tended to crack after a great deal of use. Weaponless, he started to head back up the hill for a third time when a Japanese round smacked him in the chest. He stumbled back and fell into the bottom of the gully.

From the top of the hill, Lampman saw McCarter lying in the hole by the road. From afar, he looked dead. But they weren't sure, and McCarter's unit mates refused to let him lie there exposed.

"Follow me," Lampman said to a couple of paratroopers as he dashed down toward the gully. The rest of the paratroopers peppered the trolley cars with covering fire. Bullets exploded around the gully as Lampman and the rescue party arrived. A few of the paratroopers fired back in a vain attempt to keep the Japanese heads down. Lampman grabbed McCarter by his web gear and yanked him out of the gully. He dragged him to the top of the magazine and into the large crater near the big ventilator where the mortars were set up.

Calhoun knelt down next to McCarter.

The bullet had hit McCarter in the middle of the chest, stopping near his heart. Calhoun was worried the man would soon go into shock, but despite the blood and the trauma, McCarter was calm. If anything, he was angry to be out of the fight.

"If my dad-gum gun hadn't worn out, I'd have stopped them all," McCarter said.

Calhoun took up McCarter's busted rifle and shook his head. He had never seen a split operating rod. But Calhoun didn't have time to dwell on it. He had seven wounded and the medic was out of plasma. Besides McCarter and Schilli, Aimers, who only hours before had drilled the Japanese officer through his own field glasses, was shot. Pfc. John Albersman, Pfc. Lawrence Rainville, and one of the machine gunners were also hit by Japanese fire. Calhoun needed to get them to the aid station. But it was still dark, meaning no movement. Plus, none of the wounded men could walk and needed litters. But Calhoun couldn't spare a man.

While Calhoun checked on the wounded, Staff Sergeant Johnson gathered up ammo from third squad. Bayonets were fixed again, and trench knives readied. Dawn was still a ways away, and the radio net was still closed.

"Where are those flares?"

Up on the magazine, enemy fire had every man on edge. The Japanese light machine gun from under the trolley car north of the hill kept everyone down. Pfc. Pasquale Ruggio made the mistake of standing up, and was immediately killed.

Any movement drew fire.

Calhoun went to check on the wounded several times and assured them they'd get back to the aid station and Doc Bradford as soon as they could clear a path.

"Don't worry," McCarter told Calhoun on one of his visits. "I'm doing all right."

Despite the chest wound, McCarter never went into shock. He was a tough man, and complaint was not in his vocabulary.

While Calhoun waited for another attack, Endo gathered his officers. With more than five hundred men in tow, he'd made it through to the ruins of Corregidor's noncommissioned officers' club, close to Mile Long Barracks and the regimental headquarters set up inside.

"The objective before you must be taken at all costs," Endo told his officers. "To do so, every officer and man must give his all for the emperor."

Endo drew his sword and took his position in front of the column. The sun was cresting the horizon as his men broke into a howling charge. The paratroopers on Topside were just waking up, reaching for first cigarettes or a quick breakfast, when they were greeted by a throng of screaming Japanese marines rushing across the parade field. Men who had been shaving dropped their razors and grabbed their rifles. The enemy horde crashed through American positions, trampling over surprised para-troopers as they raced toward Mile Long Barracks. The American soldiers did not remain stunned for long. Soon, cries of "Banzai" were drowned out by the roar of machine-gun fire.

A group of six marines made it to the door of the headquarters, but a sentry with a carbine stopped their charge. Colonel Jones, hearing the gunfire outside, rushed out, his pistol drawn. He shot three attackers before they could infiltrate the building.

Less than an hour after his final speech, Endo's charge was over for good. The bodies of Japanese marines were strewn across the parade field. Among the dead was Lieutenant Endo.

BACK AT BATTERY HEARN, as Endo's troops had prepared to rush the parade field, Calhoun had heard the chants start up again. His eyes shifted from the road to the sky and back again, searching for a hint of enemy movement. The situation was critical. Every paratrooper knew that there wasn't enough ammunition left to stop another attack. Finally, the first rays of light stretched across the water.

With sunrise, the radio net came to life. Calhoun snatched the mic from the radioman in his command crater and called over to Bailey.

"There are Japs between us," he said. "We are cut off to the east by the Japs in the railroad cut, and to the north by Japs under and around the trolley cars."

His men were low on ammunition, Calhoun added. The company had no way of stopping another assault.

"Roger," came Bailey's reply, crackling over the radio. "I'll alert battalion."

After Bailey signed off, Calhoun heard another message through the static. Capt. Henry "Hoot" Gibson's voice came over the net. The commander of the Battery B, 462nd Parachute Field Artillery Battalion, he had a battery of .50-caliber machine guns on Topside, several hundred yards behind Calhoun's position.

"We're looking right down the railroad," he heard Gibson say. "There's a bunch of people in that concrete railroad cut behind you. Is that you?"

Calhoun picked up the radio mic.

"No, sir," he replied, "that's the remnants of that bunch that had been attacking us."

"OK," Gibson said. "We'll take care of that."

The Japanese were hiding in between the fourteen-foot concrete walls that Calhoun's platoon had walked through the day before on their way to Battery Smith. From behind his position, Calhoun heard the thundering roar of .50-caliber machine guns. The Japanese couldn't climb out of the concrete valley—they were trapped. The gun's massive bullets tore the enemy to pieces. It was a turkey shoot.

Nearby, Sergeant Phillips and the other mortarmen searched through dozens of discarded shell cartons, finding only a half dozen mortar rounds. They fired them at the railroad cut, blasting any survivors. When the firing stopped, Calhoun sent a patrol down to the cut to check for anyone who may have some-how lived through the barrage. They arrived to find a huge bomb crater next to the wall on the far side. Phillips's mortar rounds had landed in the crater, killing a dozen Japanese soldiers who had been taking cover from the storm of .50-caliber bullets. Their corpses were so mangled that Calhoun's men couldn't get an exact body count.

The last banzai charge had been stopped before it even started.

Out of danger, Calhoun immediately organized carrying parties for the wounded. Lampman and three other paratroop-ers lifted McCarter down the hill, headed for the aid station. From the magazine's large concrete double doors emerged a Jap-anese marine, who threw a grenade at the men. His aim was poor and the grenade hit a steel pole that carried the electric wire into the magazine and dropped back on him. The paratroopers didn't wait for the explosion. They kept their heads down and headed for Topside.

With the wounded out of harm's way, Calhoun focused on eliminating the Nambu machine gun under the trolley car. He brought the bazooka team over from the west side.

"The machine gun is under the trolley car," he told the gun-ner, pointing.

The loader slid a rocket into the tube and the gunner aimed the bazooka at the turned-up floor of the car. The rocket hit square but didn't explode. The rotten wood wasn't solid enough to detonate the round. Instead, it buried itself into the hill be-hind the car.

"Hit the rails," Calhoun told the gunner.

The loader slid another rocket into place. The gunner zeroed in on the rails and fired. The rocket sailed across the road but missed. After the second rocket, the Japanese answered with a burst from the machine gun, forcing the paratroopers to duck.

The loader went back to work. But the gunner was shaken by the gunfire. He couldn't focus and missed the rail again. The miss was again answered by the machine gun.

"McDonald," Calhoun said. "Come here."

Calhoun knew Pfc. Bill McDonald was an excellent marksman.

"Yes, sir," McDonald said when he got to Calhoun.

"See that rail?" Calhoun said. "Hit it."

"I'll do my best, sir," McDonald said.

Without hesitation, McDonald took the bazooka, carefully aimed, and fired. The round hit the rail and exploded, sending shattered steel into the hidden gunner.

In the wake of the explosion, a single man staggered from the trolley car, dazed and bleeding. When he saw the paratroopers, he sat in the dirt, crossed his legs, and raised both arms above his head. He bowed several times toward Calhoun and the men on Battery Hearn.

Calhoun was baffled. Was he surrendering? He grabbed the radio mic and called over to Bailey.

"Take him alive," Bailey ordered. "Regiment desperately needs prisoners."

The intelligence officers on Topside wanted to know how many Japanese were on the island and where they were hiding.

Calhoun organized a patrol of five paratroopers led by Private

Mikel to go down to the trolley cars. But before they headed off, he warned them to hold their fire.

"One of you all is gonna get trigger-happy and want to kill him," he said.

He reminded them that men who captured a prisoner received three days of R&R—rest and relaxation—as soon as possible. For men who had endured days of intense combat under a scorching sun, there could be no better incentive.

The patrol moved out, following the trail down toward the trolley car. They were within ten yards when the Japanese gunner pulled a grenade. One of the paratroopers instantly shot him dead.

"Damn," the paratrooper said. "For a while there, I thought I had me a three-day pass."

A short while later, Mikel and two other men returned to destroy the Japanese machine guns. As they approached the trolley car, they passed a bomb crater with four Japanese marines sprawled out dead inside. They continued on, unfazed, and began to inspect the car, looking for the guns. Mikel circled off alone to look on the other side of the trolley. A few seconds later his mates heard him scream. They raced around the car to find Mikel tussling with the four "dead" marines, one of whom was trying to stuff a grenade down Mikel's shirt.

"They're alive!" Mikel shouted. "They're alive! Shoot the bastards before they kill me!"

The paratroopers opened fire, knocking the men down as Mikel broke free. When he had first seen the four Japanese, they'd been lying dead in a foxhole. Once his attention had shifted elsewhere, those four had turned out to be anything but dead. On Corregidor, a man couldn't trust even a corpse.

WHEN THE NEWS about Wheeler Point reached the aid station, Captain Bradford gathered his gear. At dawn, a squad escorted him to First Lt. Turinsky's position. Most of the casualties he found there had lost a great deal of blood, and he began at once to administer first aid.

Fourteen paratroopers had died overnight, and fifteen more were wounded. More than two hundred and fifty Japanese marines were strewn along a two-hundred-yard stretch of Cheney Trail. After that point, D Company changed the name of the area to Banzai Point.

CALHOUN WAS ANGRY when he heard what they'd lost overnight. Standing over Sergeant White's body, he realized no one at regiment even knew D and F Company had come under attack. No support had come from the ships offshore or the planes overhead.

His mind drifted back to First Lt. Campbell, who had been shot in the head while surveying Battery Wheeler a few days earlier. If the 503rd had called in support from the warplanes on Mindoro, maybe Campbell would have had a chance to get off this island and see his newborn son. White, killed the night before, would still be breathing too.

Calhoun stared down at White's face, yellow now with a waxy sheen. Tears rolled down Calhoun's cheeks.

"Damn," Calhoun said. "Damn, Donald, why'd you have to move out further to protect your squad's flank?"

The futility of the war was too much to bear. Calhoun knew the truth. Paratroopers in rifle companies were not to think before they acted, nor were Japanese marines, forced by their superiors to charge up a hill into the teeth of a machine gun. They were merely instruments of war, sent by planners to complete the mission regardless of the personal cost. A truth about fighting men that Tennyson expressed in "The Charge of the Light Brigade":

"Theirs but to do and die."

CHAPTER 14

Maggot Valley

CALHOUN GOT THE order to go back to Topside later that afternoon. His men had spent the morning destroying Japanese machine guns around Battery Hearn and now moved cautiously down the road and across the rail junctions, heading east. Near the ordnance machine shop on the back side of Way Hill, they ran into First Lt. Lee standing with a group of paratroopers. Their fatigues were salt-encrusted from days of sweat and soaked in fresh blood, flies congregating on the stickiness. Behind them, smoke poured out of the machine shop's windows and doorway.

Lee was bleeding from his scalp.

"What happened?" Calhoun asked the lieutenant.

Earlier that morning, Calhoun had sent Lee and the extra men to Way Hill, where Bailey and the rest of F Company were dug in. There, Lee's party had linked up with Bailey, and then moved back toward Topside. Rounding the east side of Way Hill, the company came upon the ordnance machine shop, which was built back into the hill, with a concrete front and solid steel windows and doors. Bailey ordered the company to stop for a break and wait for Calhoun and his platoon to catch up.

The paratroopers lay out on the ground resting, or dug into rations, or answered the call of nature. Pfc. Fred Morgan walked over to an open window of the shop and peered inside. A shot rang out, and Morgan fell dead from a bullet to the head. At once the paratroopers were alert, snatching up their weapons and pulling back from the building.

Japanese marines were clearly holed up inside, though none of the Americans had any notion of how many they were facing. To neutralize the unknown force, the paratroopers at first tried using a low-trajectory mortar, a weapon that had been developed by Norman Petzelt, a 503rd sergeant, while the regiment was back in Australia. It was a homemade contraption built from a standard mortar and designed to lob a round directly at a target so that the round would not hit the forest canopy on the way up or down. The mortar hadn't been used the night before, so the gunners had forty or fifty rounds.

Shortly, a 75mm pack howitzer arrived. The paratroopers pulled the gun down to the clearing immediately in front of the building and set it up to fire directly inside. For several minutes, they pounded the interior with howitzer shells and mortar rounds. When the firing ceased, Bailey ordered Lee to take a squad into the shop to assess the situation. After first lobbing some grenades into the confined space, Lee's squad ducked through the doorway and stepped inside.

They found a short corridor, which turned sharply to the right and emptied into a large storeroom. Hiding there, stunned by the bombardment of artillery and grenades, were twenty-seven Japanese marines. The paratroopers didn't wait for them to recover. Someone fired and the round ricocheted off the concrete walls, wounding Lee. Killing the enemy with bullets was out of the question; leaving them behind was equally unacceptable. The paratroopers drew their trench knives or raised their bayonets, and rushed the dazed Japanese. When they finally emerged from the shop into the light of day, their uniforms were drenched in blood.

After Lee finished telling his story to Calhoun, he headed off for the aid station. He was later evacuated.

With the machine shop cleared, Bailey led the company to a sloping lawn in the rear of Mile Long Barracks. They spread out on the grass near a large hedge. Calhoun heard the snap of rifle fire and the rattle of machine guns coming from nearby James Ravine. A few rounds cracked through the hedge, but no one was hit. Bullets weren't on the paratroopers' minds.

Thirst was.

They needed water. Most of their canteens were dry.

While Bailey met with the headquarters, the paratroopers fanned out, looking for water. At the center of the barracks, near the aid station and regimental headquarters, F Company found Lister bags full of water under a cluster of tall trees. The 503rd's Third Battalion had cleared the road to Bottomside, meaning the single M7 that had earlier brought the first load of water no longer had to make a mad dash through Japanese ambushes to get to Topside. Trailers were now hauling water from tanks brought over on barges to the paratroopers on Topside.

"Fill both canteens," Calhoun told his men. "Drink all you want."

The paratroopers descended on the bags, drinking until they were satisfied. After filling his canteens, Calhoun saw Emory Ball coming toward him. His best friend in the unit, Ball had been Calhoun's assistant platoon leader on New Guinea. He'd taken over the platoon while Calhoun recovered from his wounds, then moved over to E Company's mortar platoon. Ball had heard about the battle at Battery Hearn the night before and wanted to make sure his old friend survived.

Ball and Calhoun retreated to a balcony on the second floor of the barracks. Leaning against the banister, they talked and smoked for two hours. Calhoun drank a canteen of water while they talked. It was a small respite from the chaos of the night before. At one point, Ball complained about the lack of action in his new job.

"I'm practically a rear-echeloner now," Ball said. "I'm out of harm's way for the rest of the war."

After the company finally moved out, Ball and Calhoun returned to the ground floor. Before they parted, Ball put his hand on Calhoun's shoulder.

"Bill, take care of yourself," Ball said.

"You take care of yourself," Calhoun said.

"You're the one we have to worry about," Ball said. "You're the rifle platoon leader. I'm safe with my mortar platoon."

Calhoun found his men at the Corregidor lighthouse, which sat east of the parade ground overlooking the golf course. Next to the lighthouse were four large concrete water-storage tanks. Two had been destroyed by artillery fire or bombing, but the other two were still intact. Several men climbed up the iron-rung access ladders and spread out their gear, making the most of a well-earned rest. From their perch atop the tanks, under the glare of the tropical sun, they enjoyed a panoramic view of the island and the surrounding seas.

Calhoun set up his headquarters in the lighthouse. By now it was the fourth day of battle, and F Company had been in so many scrapes, and had lost so many soldiers to combat wounds, that Colonel Jones's headquarters had placed the unit in reserve. After last night's banzai charge, gaps in the perimeter were ordered closed. F Company's mission was now to plug up the line in the event of a breakthrough.

With his gear stowed in the lighthouse, Calhoun went for a walk around the area, taking in the views of the South China Sea and the long tail of the island stretching into Manila Bay. Thirst was no longer an issue. Calhoun almost felt human again. Some of his men even shaved. No longer thirsty, the paratroopers' appetites returned. They lay on the concrete tanks on their stomachs, ponchos over their heads, eating. The ponchos kept the flies away.

With no hidden tunnels or underground structures on this part of the island, the paratroopers felt secure. The sun set, and F Company slept for the first time in two days. They rested until morning, when a new mission came down from the battalion headquarters. The higher-ups wanted a body count from the fight around Battery Hearn.

The battle changed after the failed banzai charges. Planners believed the Japanese could no longer mass and attack. The paratroopers had successfully thinned their numbers, but they wanted to make sure. So far, the Americans had tabulated about 1,500 enemy dead. But two prisoners had claimed that Corregidor held more than 4,000 Japanese defenders, each one determined to kill Americans or die trying.

F Company walked back down from Topside, careful to avoid the machine shop. As they approached the area near Battery Hearn, the odor hit them: the putrid stench of decomposing bodies.

In the gully where McCarter had made his stand, Calhoun saw fly-covered, bloated bodies strewn across the trail and the hill. The corpses were crawling with maggots that undulated like ripples from a stone tossed in a pond. In some craters they found piles of limbs and torsos, so mangled and scattered that the paratroopers could only guess at how many men had died there. Estimates were made of the dead in the railway cut and crater as well. The stench and the flies made the work almost unbearable.

The paratroopers started calling the area "Maggot Valley."

With the count complete, Calhoun led the men to the top of Way Hill, where the company command post was again established. On higher ground, the smell was better. As the sun baked the bodies in the valley below, the stench grew worse. Even the sailors on the ships patrolling the island could smell it. Calhoun was happy to be out of the valley. Settled in, the paratroopers opened up rations and hoped for a quiet afternoon.

Calhoun was eating when the radio crackled to life. A second-platoon patrol was in trouble near Battery Grubbs. They had one wounded man and were taking fire from the ravine.

Calhoun got to his feet.

"Second squad," he said, getting his equipment on and gathering up the men.

Calhoun led the squad and a medic down the hill and onto Grubbs Road. They followed it to a wide trail that led into Grubbs Ravine, from which Endo had led his column during the banzai attack. As the paratroopers marched, the sound of gunfire grew louder. Calhoun spotted a bend up ahead. Just on the other side was the patrol. The paratroopers were lined up along the ridgeline, firing into the tangle of trees at the bottom of the valley.

As Calhoun and his men moved up to the edge, he spotted Pfc. Homer Patterson on the ground. Patterson, from Mississippi, was a quiet young soldier who always did his duty without complaint. He'd been shot from the ravine as the patrol walked the trail. Calhoun and the medic knelt next to him. The bullet had hit him in the right rib cage and exited through his left side under his armpit. Calhoun saw blood bubbling from the wounds.

The medic blocked the air exiting the holes with compress bandages. He cut strips of poncho and strapped them around Patterson's torso to hold the bandages in place.

197

"We need a litter," the medic told Calhoun, looking around to see what could be used to carry Patterson back to the aid station. "He needs medical help immediately."

Two paratroopers cut small saplings and stretched a poncho over the poles and snapped it together. The medic stuck a needle into Patterson's arm and started giving him plasma.

"We need to hurry," he told Calhoun.

Lampman and three paratroopers helped get Patterson on the litter.

"One, two, three . . ."

The paratroopers grabbed the saplings.

"Lift."

All four men lifted the makeshift litter and headed at a trot back toward Topside. Calhoun and the rest of the platoon followed. When they got to Grubbs Road, they headed up the valley toward the aid station.

It was a race against death.

The terrain was steep, the ground rocky and broken, and soon the litter team was spent. When one man stumbled, another would jump in without missing a step. The men scrambled in and out, passing off the litter as they made steady progress toward the aid station.

Their pace was relentless. Patterson was going to live.

Calhoun waved the radioman over and called Bailey. He told him they had one wounded man and asked him to alert the aid station. He was shot through the lungs and was losing blood. When they arrived at the edge of the parade ground, a team met them and took over the litter, scrambling off at a good clip toward the aid station, leaving the exhausted paratroopers in their wake. When Calhoun and his men got to the aid station, Captain Bradford met them at the door. Calhoun looked at him, hopeful for good news.

Bradford shook his head.

"Bill, you and your men did all you could," he said. "The wound was just too severe."

Bradford's words hit harder than Japanese bullets. They had believed they would save Patterson. They'd done everything they could to get him to the aid station. He wasn't supposed to die. The news hit the medic the hardest. Dedicated to saving lives on the battlefield, losing another paratrooper was failure, regardless of how well he did his job.

"We did everything we could," Calhoun told the medic and the rest of the men as they returned to Way Hill.

BY LATE AFTERNOON, F Company had returned to the lighthouse, once again setting up on the concrete slabs atop the water tanks. After breakfast the next morning, marking their fifth day on Corregidor, Calhoun moved his platoon out at 0800. His mission was to sweep Sunset Ridge, near Grubbs Ravine where Patterson had been mortally wounded.

The ridge was almost a vertical drop down to the South Shore Road. All day they heard other companies fighting, but Calhoun didn't find any Japanese. He was sure the Japanese were holed up in the caves in the ravines, but as his men patrolled through the brush to the waterline they didn't encounter any resistance.

On their way back to Topside, they patrolled up Grubbs Ravine. Calhoun spotted a line of trucks up ahead, and as he drew closer, he spotted bullet holes in the hoods and roofs. He looked up. Above him, the trees and vines had been stripped bare of their greenery, so the vehicles, once hidden by foliage, were now exposed to the air.

The Air Corps must have bombed and strafed them.

The paratroopers picked their way past the line of cars, clearing every corner expecting an ambush. As Calhoun passed one car, he studied the bullet holes. Air Corps strafing runs had shredded the doors and interiors. Windshields were broken and glass littered the dirt around the tires. His mind went back to his childhood, when at the Louisiana State Fair he'd seen the V-8 Ford that Clyde Barrow and Bonnie Parker had died in. Law officers had riddled the car with bullets. The back window was smashed and the interior was tattered and stained by blood splatter. Calhoun never forgot the sight of the car.

Up ahead, the paratroopers came upon a Chevrolet prewar army truck. When one man looked in the bed, he found a Japanese soldier sleeping near the foot-tall sideboards. The paratroopers jerked him off the bed and brought him over by Calhoun. They searched him and bound his hands. He was disheveled and weaponless.

But a prisoner was a prisoner.

Calhoun assigned a man to guard the Japanese soldier as the patrol continued up the ravine. Headquarters would be pleased. The patrol had made it only a few yards when the prisoner started to shout. Every man stopped in his tracks. The prisoner was giving away their position. Before the paratroopers could react, he launched himself at his guard, kicking and swinging. The paratrooper backed away as the man spit at him and continued to scream.

Everyone was looking around. They were getting nervous. Every shout alerted the Japanese in the surrounding tunnels that an American patrol was nearby. The man was growing louder by the second. Then several shots rang out. The Japanese soldier stopped shouting and crumpled to the ground, dead.

One of the paratroopers lowered his rifle. This was not a place for a commotion, especially if it drew enemy fire. They left the Japanese soldier's body next to the corpses of the cars.

CHAPTER 15

Lord, I'm Helpless

HOMER PATTERSON WAS never far from the paratroopers' minds. Two days after his death, the three platoons of F Company gathered at dawn at the head of Grubbs Ravine, which extended down between Batteries Smith and Grubbs toward the sea. Calhoun's platoon was assigned to follow the stream bed that ran the length of the ravine. Behind them, the mortar platoon would follow, ready to provide covering fire. Two flamethrower teams, as well as a demolition team to seal any tunnel entrances they encountered, rounded out Calhoun's force. The other two platoons were placed in positions along the edges of the ravine to cover Calhoun's movements in the event his men got into trouble.

Calhoun and his men waited at the head of the ravine with First Lt. Bailey as the other two platoons worked their way into position. When both platoon sergeants radioed they were ready, Calhoun looked at Bailey. Both were surprised that the platoons had reached their start positions so quickly. Bailey radioed back to double-check, but both sergeants confirmed they were in position.

"Let's go," Calhoun told his men as they started down the slope.

There was no cover near the top of the ravine. The large trees had been defoliated by the heavy bombing. The ground was littered with broken tree limbs and splintered wood debris. Sticks cracked under the paratroopers' boots as they walked forward in a long skirmish line. Visibility was good as they picked their way down what was more of a minor crease in the landscape than a true ravine.

Calhoun wiped sweat from his brow. The air was hot and muggy, but he wasn't sure if the sweat was from the heat or from the tension. He was walking into a gunfight. Everyone knew it. His only comfort was the two other platoons watching his flank. If they saw the Japanese before the ambush, they could neutralize them.

About one hundred yards down, the damage to the trees lessened and the forest canopy was intact. Calhoun could see his whole skirmish line as they approached a dry stream bed near the bottom of the ravine. The ground was rough and sloped, especially as they reached the middle of the stream. The banks were two to three feet high. February was the dry season on Corregidor, and it had probably been months since the gully had run with water.

Up ahead, Calhoun spotted a small corrugated metal building sitting on the left bank of the shallow stream bed. The building looked like a shed, about twelve feet by twelve feet. Calhoun saw his men approach it. His eyes went from the shed to a culvert in the middle of the ravine that ran under Rock Point Trail. The shallow stream bed disappeared into its shadows.

One of the paratroopers passed the shed without looking. The door was on the west side, away from the men in the stream bed. Calhoun stepped up onto the bank, with Private Mikel just behind him. Calhoun stopped at the shed and peered in. His eyes were trying to adjust to the darkness inside, searching the small space for a human form, when the whole ravine exploded in machine-gun and rifle fire.

Ambush.

Calhoun hit the ground. In the time it took to turn his head, the two men nearest him fell, and he saw blood. Mikel was closest, lying on his back, not moving, his right thigh torn open viciously, probably from a shotgun blast. He was wearing sunglasses, so Calhoun couldn't tell if the man was alive or dead. All around him, paratroopers crawled behind tree trunks or into holes.

Amid the deafening mechanical clatter of machine guns, the enemy were at once nowhere and everywhere. Dirt and debris were kicked up into the air as the Japanese laid down a base of fire. It took Calhoun a second to gather his wits. Nambu light machine guns were firing from tunnels on either side of the ravine, which F Company's supporting platoons were supposed to be covering. Heavy rifle fire was coming from the culvert ahead. Pinned down, Calhoun set up a hasty defense while paratroopers from third platoon worked their way down the valley to help.

Between bursts, Calhoun crawled toward Mikel, who was still motionless. He leaned down. "Don't you move," he said. "We'll get you out in a little while."

Nearby, Pfc. Paul Narrow had suffered gunshot wounds in both ankles. A medic rushed to his side, but a burst from a Nambu cut him down. Narrow exposed himself to fire back, getting off a few rounds before another burst killed him as well.

The paratroopers were getting chewed up.

Where are our goddamn mortars? Calhoun thought. *Where are the other platoons?* His men were under attack. Why didn't their supporting troops engage? As rounds snapped overhead, it dawned on him. The other platoons were in the wrong spot. They couldn't see his men. The only chance his men had was to get the other platoons into the fray.

Looking back, he saw the mortarmen coming down the rocky bed. He yelled for them to stop. Calhoun did not want to leave his prone position by the side of the building, but he had to get the mortars firing. He rolled over and looked at Mikel, who was still.

"I'm going to get the mortars into action," Calhoun said to him. "Don't move. I'll be back shortly."

Calhoun took a second to gather himself. Then, in one motion, he popped to his feet and tore up the stream bed. In an open field of fire, soldiers taking cover or lying prone, he was the sole moving target, and the easiest. Puffs of dirt burst up all around him as machine-gun rounds chewed up the ground, following his run. It was the second time he'd dodged his way to safety. The first time, at Battery Wheeler, had cost him one man.

Now three more were down, and he was determined not to lose any more.

Back near the shed, Mikel, in pain and likely going into shock from loss of blood, sat up to examine his thigh wound, when several bullets from the culvert smacked into his chest. He fell back into the stream bed and didn't move.

Calhoun reached the safety of the mortar team's position unscathed, and quickly had the crews lobbing shells toward the culvert and Rock Point Trail. With the mortars in action, Calhoun raced back down the ravine. The gunfire grew louder as he got close to the shed. He could hear the call and response of American and Japanese fire as both sides battled. Then he heard American .30-caliber machine guns open up from the flanks. The other two platoons were engaged.

Up on the bank, Pfc. James Wilson, second squad's first scout, crawled forward, but stopped when he heard Japanese voices coming from inside the culvert. He pulled the pin on a phosphorus grenade, reached over the bank's edge, and tossed it into the culvert. He waited for it to blow, then leapt over the bank and opened fire with his Thompson submachine gun, raking the opening with bullets. As smoke poured out of the culvert, Japanese defenders rushed out, only to be met with volleys of fire from the paratroopers. Wilson's attack broke the back of the ambush. The other Japanese defenders disappeared into the safety of the tunnels and the paratroopers charged forward. When Calhoun got to the culvert later, he counted eight dead Japanese piled up in and around the opening.

To his left, Calhoun saw Pfc. Theodore Yocum crossing the

ravine with Pfc. James Bradley. They were racing toward cover when Yocum called out just as a Japanese soldier ahead of them popped up and opened fire.

"Bradley, look out!"

Bradley ducked. The bullets hit Yocum, who fell to the ground and pulled his legs up into the fetal position. His body relaxed and he died.

There had been more Japanese than just this lot. Where had the remainder gone? Just beyond where Rock Point Trail crossed the culvert, on the southern side, Private Lampman's sharp eye spotted a concealed tunnel entrance, covered by brush. Where there's one tunnel, there's more than likely to be two. Sure enough, less than twenty yards beyond, there was a second entrance farther along the trail. As the paratroopers got close to the openings, a shower of potato-masher concussion grenades came flying out of the two openings. The grenades landed short and exploded harmlessly.

Calhoun called up the demolition team. They placed charges at the mouth and set them off. The explosion was massive, almost killing one member of the demolition team huddled nearby. Debris shot up into the air and the bank gave way, sending cascades of dirt down the side of the ravine.

A Japanese machine gun on the right flank drew Calhoun's attention. His first squad was under fire and he raced to their position to coordinate a counterattack. Above the second tunnel, F Company's second platoon started down the side of the ravine to attack from the top. Demolition teams swung satchel charges into the entrance. The explosions forced the Japanese deeper into the tunnel. One of the flamethrower teams moved up and sprayed the entrance with fluid from four tanks. The paratroopers pulled back and the operator hit the igniter on the fifth and final flamethrower tank. A stream of flame shot out of the nozzle, turning the tunnel mouth into an inferno. The operator hosed the openings. It looked like a dragon's breath.

The fire turned the tunnels into ovens. Heat rolled off in waves and thick black smoke rose into the air. The paratroopers found cover and waited. Soon they saw movement, and then Japanese defenders darted out from the fiery mouth, some with their uniforms ablaze. From behind a tree, Lampman shot them down with his BAR, with other paratroopers adding to the barrage. It was merciful gunfire, as all of the Japanese were in agony, wounded or burning, by the time they exited the mouth of the tunnel.

The paratroopers made sure the tunnel was clear and blew the entrance closed. With the ravine raked clean of enemy troops, F Company headed back toward Topside. Bailey sent Calhoun's unit back to the lighthouse. They were beat up again and needed to refit and rest. The men collapsed all around the water tanks. Calhoun stowed his gear and worked his way up to the lighthouse's catwalk. He wanted to be alone.

OVER THE LAST five days, Captain Bradford had noticed the paratroopers had grown accustomed to facing death. The loss of a friend to enemy fire no longer rattled a man the way it had the morning they dropped onto Corregidor. Nothing illustrated the point better than the story of a skirmish near Monkey Point, which sat on the south side of the island's tail. Bradford heard that a company there had come under sniper fire and managed to pinpoint the shooter's location, peppering him with gunfire and grenades. They assumed the sniper was finished off. But an hour later, as the men rested nearby, a shot rang out, and Sgt. Andrew Maricic dropped dead behind a bunch of sandbags, a bullet hole in his head.

None of the men around him showed much emotion. They had trained with him, bunked with him, jumped with him, and fought beside him. But to evacuate his body would mean putting their own lives at risk. The sniper was still lurking somewhere, and others could be nearby. The platoon sergeant ordered his men to move out. They took Maricic's Thompson submachine gun, his ammo, and a pair of grenades.

Maricic was left behind to lie dead under the tropical sun.

A week later, Bradford ran into one of Maricic's friends at the aid station. He'd heard about Maricic's death and told him what a fine man he was.

"Yes," the soldier replied, "and you know, I can't get over us leaving him behind. Of course, we had to, but sometimes at night now, right when I'm sleeping, he comes to me as real as life, complaining that I'd left him behind with the Japs. Even when I wake up, his voice is in my mind just like we'd been talking together, but of course it goes away. Then I light a cigarette and smoke it out, and go to sleep again."

To the outside world, it looked heartless. But Bradford knew it was something else.

"Death had become a familiar member of this and every other squad," he wrote later. "There was no time for sentiment."

ATOP THE LIGHTHOUSE, sitting on the catwalk, Calhoun stared off past Corregidor's jagged tail at the hazy blue horizon, his mind drifting back to Texas, and Sarah Joe, the young wife he had left behind. When he jumped from the door of his C-47 five days earlier, he had no doubts that he'd one day return home to her embrace. But after today's fighting, Calhoun wasn't so sure. Doubt, like the coming night, had begun to creep into his mind. He'd tempted fate already. On that first night, he'd been on the lip of the crater facing Battery Wheeler. When he left to give instructions to the bazooka gunner, Thomas had replaced him, and was killed. It just as easily could have been him. On the third night, dug in on the hill above Battery Hearn, he'd sur- vived wave after wave of fanatical Japanese. So many men had died, but he had walked away without a scratch. But for how long could he go on?

His platoon had been hit hard, but other men from F Com- pany were dead too. Second Lt. Clifford MacKenzie had plunged into the kill zone of a Japanese machine gun near Way Hill to help two trapped men and was cut down. Calhoun thought of his last memory of MacKenzie, laughing and talking to buddies as he waited to follow his platoon.

The absence of familiar faces was piling up. Lopez. White. Patterson. Flash. McCarter. While the Americans were slowly whittling down the Japanese defenses, the battlefield was catching up with the weary soldiers. The cost was felt by every man who walked Corregidor.

Now today. Calhoun had lost three men. Narrow. Yocum. Mikel.

He thought of Mikel and all the things he had read in the man's letters home. He thought of Mikel's infant son—one he'd never meet—and the love he had expressed to his wife. And he thought of the sacrifices the man had made for his new family, even accepting a cut in rank to avoid being shipped home to the United States, a world away from his wife and son in Australia. To make extra cash, Mikel had collected Japanese artifacts and sold them to Army Air Corps soldiers and rear-base men. He had managed to earn 800 Philippine pesos, about $400, which he tucked away in the breast pocket of his fatigues. He once asked Calhoun to see that his wife got the money, as well as a Leica camera he prized, if he were killed in action. Mikel also asked him to get his $10,000 insurance policy paid out to her and not to his sister, even though they both knew it could not be done. Now Calhoun vowed to keep his promise. One or two more steps in that firefight, and he could have ended up dead instead of Mikel. Why had he felt compelled to look into the metal building?

Calhoun had long ago given up trying to understand the war. To some, who lived and who died was simply chance or even dumb luck. But Calhoun rejected the randomness of war. His answer to why some lived and some died was simple.

God.

It was God's blessing that kept him alive.

There, on the lighthouse's catwalk, he put his hands together and gazed to the heavens. He'd abandoned lengthy prayers by this point. Now when he talked to God, it was one simple statement.

"Lord, I'm helpless. If you want me, take me to be with you."

CHAPTER 16

Ball's Razor

THE NEXT MORNING, while First Lt. Bailey set up a command post on Way Hill, Calhoun and the rest of F Company headed back to Battery Smith. When they arrived, Calhoun sent one squad to the top of the battery's magazine to serve as a lookout, and another into the tunnel that led from Maggot Valley directly into the magazine. Spearheading the third squad, Calhoun led his men into the magazine from the gun side on the west.

They found themselves in a concrete tunnel lined with Japanese knapsacks, like soldiers in formation. The paratroopers rifled through them, finding clothes, prayer sashes, and battle flags. The tunnel opened into a large room with a door in the rear, which led to another magazine room. As Calhoun looked over the room, he began noticing small fabric envelopes, which he guessed their owners wore suspended from a string around their necks. Inside he found postcards, snapshots, and prayers written in Japanese script. The photographs showed soldiers in training, teenagers dressed in uniforms carrying wooden rifles, and then the same faces, now grown men, with real rifles. Their uniforms bore the insignia of the Imperial Japanese Navy.

The room was big enough to shelter five hundred men, he estimated. He couldn't help but think back a few nights, when he was almost forced to set up on top of this magazine in the face of countless enemy attackers. Were even more Japanese marines hiding underneath his men as they fought off the banzai charges?

The thought gave him chills.

While the paratroopers took souvenirs, Calhoun went out to the concrete platform in front of the magazine and called Bailey on the radio. He told him about the packs and his estimate of Japanese forces at Battery Smith.

After a full day of patrolling, the company reassembled near Way Hill and moved back to their bivouac area around the lighthouse. It was a quiet day for Calhoun.

But the paratroopers in E Company on the road to Battery Monja at Wheeler Point were fighting for their lives.

THAT MORNING, AS Calhoun left for Battery Smith, his best friend, Emory Ball, shaved. His men used the razor first. When it was finally his turn, he took the razor and smiled.

"Officers who shave before an action always get killed," he said.

But he didn't believe it. He was in no danger, something he and Calhoun had talked about when they met at the barracks.

His mortar platoon was at the top of Wheeler Point, by now far from the action. His job was to provide fire support to the rifle companies, not patrol with them.

That morning, E Company was ordered to go down Crockett Ravine to the South Shore Road and sweep the path to Battery Monja, which sat at the base of Wheeler Point. Before they left, First Lt. Roscoe Corder came looking for a forward observer. E Company needed someone to accompany them on patrol and call in mortar fire in the event they got into a scrape.

Ball volunteered. He'd been itching to get out on patrol and contribute to the effort. He grabbed his weapon and helmet and followed the paratroopers, including Doc Bradford, who liked to walk patrols when things were slow in the aid station, down into Crockett Ravine.

Corder's platoon encountered no enemy fire as they moved down to the South Shore Road. They stopped at a convertible abandoned along the road leading to Battery Monja. Corder set up security at the vehicle, with paratroopers covering each direction as a platoon from E Company moved down to the beach.

As the paratroopers patrolled the waterline, Corder and Ball scanned the cliffs, searching for snipers. They spotted two tunnel entrances cut side by side into the cliff face, as well as several caves. The tunnels were Battery Monja's casement entrances. Near a cave farther up the beach, Corder spotted a Japanese marine. He shouldered his carbine and fired, killing the man. The shots made Ball jump. Ball was upset, but not because he was startled.

"I haven't had a chance to fire a shot," he told Corder.

With C Company past their position, Corder moved his platoon closer to Battery Monja and the caves. There was no cover as they approached the entrance to the first tunnel. Naval gunfire was requested. The attack started offshore. A destroyer fired on the tunnel and caves for ten minutes. The road was covered with debris where the asphalt was torn up by shelling. Corder's platoon approached the tunnel. The paratroopers stepped over bloated Japanese bodies as they advanced.

Corder's men threw phosphorus grenades into the mouth. Smoke started to pour out and then out came the phosphorus grenade. It exploded harmlessly outside the tunnel, and the smoke filled only the mouth. From the lip of the tunnel, the paratroopers saw Japanese defenders moving.

Corder was watching the action from farther down the road and grabbed his radio.

"Hold the grenades a couple of seconds," he told the paratroopers at the mouth of the cave. "Then throw them in."

He watched one of his men pull the pin to a phosphorus grenade and wait one second. Then another second. After a third second, he threw the grenade into the cave. A second grenade went into the cave just as a pair of Japanese rushed out throwing hand grenades. The Japanese were blinded coming out of the dark tunnel into the tropical afternoon sun and their hand grenades sailed over the paratroopers. The paratroopers killed them in a barrage of fire. The rest of the platoon crowded around the front of the cave and pumped clips and magazines into the opening.

Corder called up his machine guns as he and Ball waited at a curve in the road with his radio operator and a few men from his platoon. The rest of the platoon was still clearing out the first tunnel or coming up the road. Once they went around the curve, they were in full view of the battery, and Corder wasn't going to take any chances, especially after running into Japanese in the surrounding tunnels.

When the machine guns were in place, Corder and his small group moved around the bend only to run into a massive mound of volcanic rock and dirt blocking the road. Naval gunfire had collapsed part of the cliff behind the battery. The platoon's scouts were climbing to the top of the pile, and Corder and Ball followed. From the top of the mound, they could see the entrance to the tunnel leading to the battery. One of the scouts pulled the pin of a grenade.

One, one thousand.

Two, one thousand.

Three, one thousand.

The paratrooper tossed the grenade into the mouth of the tunnel and it exploded with a muffled thump. A Japanese machine gun on the cliff above opened fire. Corder, Ball, and the others took cover. The radio operator rushed forward to get to Corder, but a machine-gun round hit a sapling in front of him and shattered the trunk. He dove for cover, snapping the radio's antenna. The small group of paratroopers on the mound had no way to call for help.

Pfc. William Brown and Pfc. Howard Jandro, carrying a BAR, rushed from the top of the mound to the entrance of the tunnel to try to break the deadlock. They were almost at the blast wall in front of the mouth when fourteen Japanese marines rushed out, throwing grenades and shouting. None of them had firearms. One marine snatched Jandro's helmet and smashed him in the face with it repeatedly. A Japanese officer attacked Brown with a *guntō*, a Japanese military sword, slashing into his face and torso.

The other paratroopers charged in, firing from the hip. A massive melee ensued, with the paratroopers' rifles quickly becoming clubs.

Pfc. Joseph Cubbage charged off the dirt mound and fired a rifle grenade into the tunnel as he approached the melee. After Brown went down, seriously wounded, the Japanese officer rushed toward Cubbage, who pointed his rifle and pulled the trigger.

Nothing happened. The rifle was jammed.

The Japanese officer kept coming. In a flash, Cubbage remembered that a rifle grenade used a blank to fire, but blanks weren't strong enough to eject on their own. He jerked back the bolt, manually ejected the blank, and threw the bolt forward, sliding a live round into the chamber. He leveled his rifle and fired, knocking the officer back with several shots.

The paratroopers wrestled Jandro and Brown free and retreated to the mound with the other paratroopers.

With the Japanese soldiers killed or wounded, there was another lull.

A phosphorus grenade soared into the mouth of the tunnel.

"What are you doing?" Corder snapped. "You shouldn't have done that."

Smoke poured out of the tunnel, and through the haze Corder spotted the shadows of men moving. He looked over his shoulder. The rest of his platoon was strung out along the road and would be no help if the Japanese rushed out. He turned back toward the mouth of the tunnel just as another wave of Japanese defenders tore out of the smoke, this time with rifles and machine guns blazing.

At the top of the mound, Corder, Ball, and the radio operator returned fire at the oncoming enemy. Ball raised himself up for a quick look and took two bullets to the chest and stomach, dust flying from the back of his fatigues as the bullets exited. He slumped down on the dirt mound beside Corder. For a moment the two men made eye contact, and then nothing.

Ball was dead.

From the mouth of the tunnel, the Japanese marines kept firing. Private Jandro, still dazed from his beating, took five bullets to the chest and fell next to Ball.

A handful of Corder's platoon made it past the second cave entrance and onto the mound. Bradford was farther back with the rest of the platoon, and now came forward to Corder's position after hearing word of casualties. He checked Ball first, then moved on to Jandro. Only Brown was alive, but mortally wounded with deep gashes from the sword.

"He needs immediate aid," Bradford said.

Cubbage picked Brown up in his arms and carried him down the road on the run. Brown died three days later.

The firing continued. Corder checked the magazine of his carbine. He had two rounds left.

"Ammo check!" he shouted over the gunfire.

The rest of the paratroopers were low on ammunition. With Brown and Cubbage gone, only Corder, his radioman, and the scouts were on the mound. The rest had already pulled back. Corder gave the order to follow. As they rushed back down the road, they had to leave the bodies of Ball and Jandro.

Farther down the road, the company dug in for the night. One of the paratroopers came up to Corder after the fight and showed him his rifle. A bullet had plowed into the wooden stock and exited through the metal butt plate.

"See how lucky I was, Lieutenant?" the paratrooper said.

Corder looked at the rifle, then at the man. "You don't know how lucky you really were. Take off your helmet."

The paratrooper swept it off his head and saw a bullet hole where the helmet and chin strap met. A few inches away and he would have been like Ball or Jandro.

That night, Corder fell asleep quickly. He was exhausted after the fighting. About midnight, Ball appeared to Corder in a dream.

"Why did you leave my body down with the Japs?" Ball said.

The dream ended before Corder could answer.

The next morning, the paratroopers sent patrols to the mound, but both Jandro and Ball were gone. The bodies were never recovered. Carted away by the Japanese with the other corpses, most likely. The next night, Ball was back in Corder's dreams with the same question.

Corder still didn't have an answer.

CHAPTER 17

Tojo Can Eat Shit

WHEN CAPTAIN BRADFORD caught up to the men of D Company, they were spread out in a defensive line near the top of the ridge that overlooked Grubbs Ravine. Machine guns with interlocking fields of fire had been set up on the flanks, just in case the Japanese decided to charge up the road again. Most of the men were dug into craters and gullies instead of foxholes—the granitelike soil of Corregidor was too difficult to dig in. Others used debris for cover. It was getting dark and the paratroopers were laying out grenades and extra magazines for easy access if they were attacked.

"Hell, Charlie, they could march a Jap army up that gulch, and they'd never cross a line fifty yards in front of us, not unless dead men can run," First Lt. Henry L. Buchanan, D Company commander, said as he stood with Bradford overlooking the line. "But we're figuring on making suicide even easier for 'em. Every five or ten minutes we drop some mortar shells in there, just scatter 'em around so's the Japs that are looking to be banzai'd can get it without coming all the way. The guns are registered in all down that trail. We'll give 'em a barrage at dawn before we move out, but the Japs can have it earlier if they ask for it."

Earlier that day, Major Caskey, Second Battalion's commander, had asked Bradford if he wanted to go on a mission from Topside to the beach at Rocky Point. D Company was going to follow the same path the Japanese used on their banzai attack against Battery Hearn a few days before. "Better spend the night with them on the perimeter," Caskey had told Bradford. "They'll be heading off early in the morning."

Now standing among D Company, Bradford noticed the difference in his uniform compared to the ones these men wore. His was not clean by normal standards, but next to paratroopers who had spent days on the front line of combat, he was sparkling. The toil of battle and living in the field could be seen on their shirts and pants, torn and stiff from dirt, blood, and sweat. Despite their grimy appearance, spirits were high. Bradford was surprised to see them cheerful, joking among the ranks as they went about their duty.

Bradford looked for a spot to sleep in a small concrete shed that had been commandeered by the company as a headquarters. It had no roof or even furniture, and the men inside had stretched out on the hard concrete floor. In the center of the front wall, a shell fragment had torn open a hole, beside which one of the men bedded down with his Thompson submachine gun lying at the ready. Machine guns were mounted in window spaces. A Japanese machine gun sat on the floor nearby.

"I got numerous ammunition," Cpl. Kenneth Combes told Bradford. "But the way of it is, that when you've got it, you don't need it, and vises versus."

"Vice versa, you mean," his sergeant corrected.

Combes smiled and winked at Bradford.

"Here, come over against the wall." The sergeant indicated toward a silky parachute bed with a pack for a pillow. "All the comforts of home, Captain," the sergeant said. "Lay down and stay with us."

Bradford knew some of these men, and their invitation was on par with the "hospitality of the Ritz" in the field. He settled down onto the makeshift bed. Nearby, paratroopers were getting ready for the darkness that would soon descend on Corregidor. Each man prepared his weapons. Bradford watched one paratrooper drop four grenades into a helmet beside his head.

"Them hand grenades is life savers," he said, pointing to one of the side windows. "There was two Nips got right outside here and were almost jumping in on us. You should have heard the beggars squeal when I gave 'em a grenade."

A blanket of darkness soon covered the area, and the men, now in place for the night, were stretched out on the floor of the shed. They passed the time by telling Bradford about the banzai attack a few nights before. Each man had his own story, but they were all similar. The Japanese had made it out of the ravine, bypassing Calhoun at Battery Hearn and sneaking past D Company at Banzai Point. When the Japanese got to the shed, they surrounded it. But American firepower had overwhelmed them.

"I wouldn't want to play on their team," one paratrooper said.

"They don't know no rules except follow the leader and get blown up."

Their conversation was interrupted by a crash and then an explosion. Bradford jumped up, but the men around him were still.

"That's Jim," the sergeant said. "His squad is on the mortars tonight. You can see the bursts out of this window, Captain. He's been landing them down in front here."

The thump of the mortar continued as rounds flew in a high arc over the American line. Bradford took up a position in the window and saw the flash like a bolt of lightning as the shells landed about sixty yards down in the ravine. He returned to his bed, but just as he was drifting off to sleep, a burst from the machine gun on the right flank jarred him awake.

"Bluey's zeroing in his guns," the sergeant said. "He always does that at dark; it's his way of saying good night."

Later on, the artillery on Topside fired a few shells. Bradford heard the rounds rustle like fluttering silk sheets overhead and felt the shudder as they hit the target area. No one stirred in the shed.

Now awake, Bradford lay on his parachute bed and listened to Combes snore. It only happened when he slept on his right side. A breeze forced Bradford and the others to pull their parachute silk up for warmth.

In the morning, he woke to a soft and spotless blue sky. *God's in his heaven, all's right with the world,* Bradford thought, a verse embedded in his head from his school days.

Everyone had slept fully clothed, and all around him paratroopers began pulling on their boots and scarfing down quick breakfasts of canned ham and eggs out of the Ten-in-One rations issued to each squad. Within minutes of sunrise, the men were all assembled outside, ready for their mission, puffing on cigarettes and awaiting orders.

First Lt. Henry Buchanan looked at his watch.

Everything kicked off with a barrage of artillery, like rolling thunder from a storm, guns pounding the ravine with volley after volley. Bradford watched the explosions in the distance. It was like a great, unseen fist smashing the ground. He could feel the earth shudder in his gut, and his whole body tingled. Down below, the rounds from the destroyers turned the ravine into a hellscape of shrapnel. After ten minutes, a silence fell over the ravine.

Buchanan, standing near the lead squad, motioned with his arm to move forward.

"Move out," he said.

The paratroopers, their weapons cradled in their arms, started down the valley. To Bradford, they looked unorganized and casual, like they were just going on a hike. But soon he saw how they moved into formation—a staggered line spaced out so a machine gunner couldn't easily get more than one man, and so their own machine guns could move up and cover as needed. The formation changed based on the terrain. Bradford marveled at how the whole company moved like a single animal. The men had an unspoken rapport as they covered one another. Even those who carried the more cumbersome weapons, like machine guns, bazookas, and flamethrowers, moved with ease over the rocky, jagged ground.

The trail cut around the shoulder of a steep hill covered in trees and underbrush. On the other side, the ravine opened up into a series of gullies. Buchanan, in the lead, halted the company and took out his field glasses.

"Better take no chances," he whispered as he scanned ahead.

He called over to the first-platoon leader, "Hold your men here while I bring up the mortars."

Bradford heard the order passed up the line and soon the mortarmen came down to Buchanan's position. They had smiles on their faces, happy to be called to action.

"We lug these condemnable things from here to next Friday, and only once in a dog's existence do they let us use 'em," a mortarman had once told Bradford. "There's all kinds of ways in and out of hell to punish men for their sins, and then there's the mortar squad."

The mortar crew set down the forty-pound baseplate in a crater and set up the tube. The ammo bearer laid out the ammunition packs.

"Hang it. Fire!"

The black speck rocketed out of the tube, high into the blue sky. Bradford tracked it like a center fielder. When it reached its zenith, it turned and like a dive bomber headed for the target. Fourteen seconds from the thump, Bradford saw the flash and then smoke from the explosion.

"Give 'em a couple more for good luck," Buchanan said. Then belayed the order. "No, hold where you are," he said. "I don't guess anyone was down there. Jim, take your squad ahead and watch out. Wait for us at the next switchback around the bend. I'm going to cover from here with machine guns."

He then turned to his radioman: "Tell the third platoon we want them forward."

With everyone in place, the company moved forward again along the zigzagging trail. Despite being in a ravine where a Japanese ambush could come at any bend, the men weren't tense. They seemed almost uninterested, but only to the untrained eye. Bradford knew a paratrooper doesn't miss much on a patrol. Every boulder was scrutinized. Each turn was inspected for a possible ambush. A paratrooper's mind was constantly doing the battlefield calculus.

They were hunters being hunted.

"You could go right by a dozen Nips in this country and never know it," one paratrooper told Bradford during a halt. "If you weren't watching, they'd come out from behind at you, and get you in the back."

The patrol was getting close to the bottom of the ravine, the trail widening out. So far, any Japanese in the vicinity were either hidden or had escaped. Bradford thought they may have left after the artillery barrage. Then, from beyond the crest of the next hill, he heard gunfire.

"There's going to be Japs down here, all right," a platoon leader told Bradford. "And the lieutenant ain't taking no chances on getting us ambushed."

Bradford looked ahead, seeing that the ravine ended in a steep drop-off into the sea. He spotted tunnels burrowed into the rock face on either side of the trail. Concrete machine-gun emplacements, built by the American Army to defend against an amphibious invasion, were set up facing the beach.

"Hold on here," Buchanan ordered his men. "We'll take a fifteen-minute break and you men rest up. I'm going to look the situation over."

As the paratroopers rested, the lieutenant scanned the end of the trail, looking for anything that might provide an advantage. He put a machine-gun team where it could cover the company's descent and told one of his squads to climb back up the trail and provide a rear guard in case they had missed some Japanese on their way down. When it was time to proceed, he joined his first platoon in the front.

"OK, boys, we'll go down and dig 'em out if there's any Nips down there," he said.

As they approached one of the machine-gun emplacements, a lookout on the hillside spotted a Japanese defender run into a nearby tunnel. They found the entrance and tossed grenades into the mouth, followed by phosphorus grenades. Then a paratrooper with a Thompson sprayed the entrance. Finally, another phosphorus grenade was tossed inside. The final grenade must have ignited some ammunition—the paratroopers saw flames, and then thick black smoke poured out of the tunnel like a chimney.

Three Japanese marines came tearing out.

One died as he landed in the dirt. The other two were badly burned. One was on fire and stumbled down the trail, while the other let out a shrill "banzai" and charged. It didn't sound like a challenge to Bradford, more of a rallying cry, a last surge of courage as he attacked.

"Banzai! Banzai!" the man shouted as he rushed forward into a volley of fire from the paratroopers.

The Japanese marine on the trail was kicking his smoking limbs. The phosphorus burned through his feet and legs. His flesh looked like black bacon. The stink of burning flesh hung in the air. It got worse near the tunnel, suggesting to Bradford other Japanese soldiers were burning within the darkness.

The company continued down the trail and took up a position about fifty feet above the sea. The Japanese had built an embankment with barbed wire across the trail's end. It was mined, and machine-gun nests with good cover were set up to defend the beach. Rough caves were cut into both sides of the trail by the ocean. The crevices formed favorable hiding places.

Buchanan led a squad to the end of the trail and around the nose of a rocky point and onto the beach near Wheeler Point. He wanted to clear a deep cleft leading up from the beach. When the squad got to a large boulder overlooking the cleft, they spotted a group of Japanese marines near the mouth of a cave. Corporal Combes opened fire, and the Japanese responded, hitting him in the chest. Combes fell back into the water at the shore. As Bradford scrambled toward him, he saw Combes's limp body get picked up by a wave and washed back among the rocks.

A paratrooper threw a grenade over the boulder, but the Japanese picked it up and threw it back. The grenade exploded, peppering the squad with shrapnel. A shard sliced through

Buchanan's helmet and thigh, knocking him down the rocks. The company medic took a piece of shrapnel in the arm, but ignored his wound and ran to Buchanan.

The rest of the squad poured fire into the cave's mouth. One of the paratroopers had learned some Japanese, and called for the men to surrender. A Japanese soldier responded in English.

"Fuck Roosevelt!"

"Tojo can eat shit!" someone shouted back, referring to Japan's prime minister. "Show your heads up and we'll blow 'em off for you."

Meanwhile, Bradford saw that there was nothing he could do for Combes. The corporal was dead. Bradford made his way back to the boulder, where the paratroopers were still exchanging fire with the Japanese.

"Reckon they is getting sick of us all, even if they isn't dead," said a paratrooper, who smiled, a contrast to the ferocity of the occasion.

The Japanese were trapped. The paratroopers dug in while Buchanan and the medic were evacuated. A Thompson machine gunner hosed the entrance of the cave with several bursts, and another phosphorus grenade was tossed in, its white plume of smoke spraying out in the darkness.

Two Japanese defenders ran out of the cave.

"Watch out!" a paratrooper yelled. "Here they come."

The two barely took a few steps into the open before they collapsed in the dirt, their arms and legs awkwardly spread out. Heavy explosions thundered within the cave itself, followed by a series of groans and howls that rapidly died out.

Then silence.

The Thompson gunner stood in the mouth of the cave and fired long bursts inside before advancing. He stepped over four bodies near the entrance and then found nineteen mangled corpses inside.

Bradford retreated to the beach to check on the wounded. A barge plowed into the cove and dropped its ramp down on the rocks ten yards from the shore. Bradford and some others waded out to it, stumbling in the surf, with Combes's body, and then returned to the vessel with the wounded medic and Buchanan.

"Watch out on the way back," the lieutenant warned as the paratroopers headed back to shore. "Some of those suckers could still be laying [in wait] for you up there."

One platoon leader waved to Buchanan as the ramp rose up.

"You watch out for those nurses back in the hospital," he said.

A grin spread across Buchanan's face as the barge's engines revved and it slowly backed off the shore. Bradford grabbed his equipment and followed the others back up the ravine to Topside.

CHAPTER 18

A Tumbling Can

AFTER TEN DAYS of combat, the battle had become for Calhoun a routine of short patrols and paperwork. The US Army was still a massive bureaucracy, and officers were required to write after-action reports and keep up with their other administrative duties. With the fighting moving toward the island's tail, Calhoun's area of operations around Topside was quiet, allowing him to catch up on paperwork.

A lack of fighting left the men with more time to explore Corregidor's labyrinth of mysteries. In some tunnels, the paratroopers discovered a treasure trove of clothing, alcohol, tools, and other goods, there for the taking. Valuables went first, then the booze, though the men soon learned not to get too excited about a cache of sake or whiskey, for officers tended to make those stores off-limits.

Among the most coveted items were clothes. The days of combat had stained uniforms with blood and sweat. Sleeves and pant legs had been torn by brambles, rocks, or gunfire. After the Japanese had taken Manila back in 1942, the contents of many of the city's clothing stores found their way onto Corregidor to await shipment back to Japan. When Calhoun's men found a cache of clothes, they rifled through the selection. Suits. Shirts. Even large rolls of fabric. Soon Calhoun spotted men in fresh slacks and button-down shirts lounging around the lighthouse. Even he got into the act, swapping out his fatigues for a yellow shirt and blue pants. But when an officer from the regimental headquarters spotted first platoon going on patrol wearing civilian clothes under their rifle belts and ammo pouches, they were ordered back into their dirty fatigues.

ONE OF CALHOUN's first duties was writing award recommendations for his men. There were a few Silver Stars and Bronze Stars with V devices for valor, but none of these were enough for Lloyd McCarter. Calhoun thought the private deserved the Congressional Medal of Honor, so he wrote a recommendation and turned it in to First Lt. Bailey. The next day, he got an order to report to Lt. Col. John Britten, the regimental executive officer. When he got to Britten's office, the man seemed irritated. Calhoun knew Britten and considered him a friend. He wasn't sure why Britten was agitated.

"You used bad judgment here," Britten said, referring to Calhoun's recommendation for McCarter. "I'm reducing it to a recommendation for a Distinguished Service Cross."

Calhoun shook his head.

"You want to go down to Maggot Valley?" Calhoun asked. "I'll go over McCarter's action in detail on the grounds where it took place."

If Britten was agitated before, now he was mad.

"Don't question my decision," he snapped. "Any more argument out of you, and the recommendation will be reduced to one for a Silver Star medal."

Calhoun swallowed his rage. Any respect for Britten was gone.

"Yes, sir," he said, saluted, and left the office.

What Calhoun didn't know was that Bailey had already been in to see Colonel Jones about the recommendation and received a similar reception. No "fuck-up" like McCarter, Jones told Bailey, was going to get the Medal of Honor in his outfit. He had already rejected a similar recommendation for Sgt. Ray E. Eubanks, who had died attacking an enemy machine gun in New Guinea with his BAR, using the gun as a club and killing nineteen Japanese in total. Despite the soldier's incredible valor, Jones reduced his recommendation to a Distinguished Service Cross. In Jones's eyes, most of the men in his regiment were citizen soldiers who didn't value awards like professional soldiers such as himself. Recommendations for both Distinguished Service Crosses and Medals of Honor were forwarded to the awards board at the US Army Forces in the Far East. They overturned Eubanks's denial and awarded him the Medal of Honor posthumously.

After the war, Jones expressed regret to one of the former paratroopers in his command. "I think I was stingy in the awarding of medals for heroic action in combat against the enemy," Jones said. "If I had known how generous other combat commanders in other units were in recognizing the actions reported by field commanders, I would have been more generous."

DURING THE SIEGE in 1942, Americans had huddled underground to escape Japanese bombs and shells. Now, three years later, underground was the last refuge for the Japanese defenders. The battle for Corregidor was coming to an end. After a spectacular parachute assault and amphibious invasion, the fighting was now mostly just skirmishes outside of tunnels. But even though victory was out of reach, the Japanese never surrendered.

Even the rare prisoner never stopped fighting.

One Japanese soldier was dragged from a hole and taken to Topside for interrogation, still struggling against the paratroopers with each step when Bradford saw him. He was brought to the regimental command post. When an American interpreter stepped forward to question him, the prisoner flung himself at the man. The officer who had brought him in hit the prisoner with a sharp uppercut, and, as he fell, kicked him in the head, killing him.

"Perhaps this was not a gentlemanly thing to do," Bradford wrote later, "but for many American soldiers the war ceased being gentlemanly when the Japs started it at Pearl Harbor. Extermination was of their own choosing."

———

IN THE MIDDLE of the island, near the base of Corregidor's long tail, soldiers from the Thirty-Fourth Infantry Regiment had occupied the top of Malinta Hill. Below them, in the labyrinth of tunnels that had once housed the remnants of General MacArthur's command in the wake of the Japanese invasion, the conquerors of Corregidor were now trapped like rats. At night, they would slip out and attack their American enemy suddenly, only to disappear back inside. The soldiers attempted to flush them out by dropping smoke grenades down the airshafts or pouring gasoline down the air vents and igniting it. Yet no matter what they tried, the Japanese refused to surrender.

Colonel Jones and Lt. Col. Edward Postlethwait, commander of the Thirty-Fourth's Third Battalion, figured there were a large number of Japanese holed up in the tunnels. A naval barrage caused a landslide that sealed the east entrance of the complex, and now Jones and Postlethwait expected that the Japanese commanders inside were planning to try to break out of the west end.

Inside Malinta Tunnel, Yoshiharu Nonaka helped drag the last of the massive gunpowder bags into the communication tunnel. It joined the countless other bags, in addition to over 100,000 artillery and mortar shells, nearly 100,000 grenades, thousands of antitank mines, and millions of rounds of small-arms ammunition, all squirreled away throughout the complex's laterals. The plan was to blow an escape route on the eastern end of Malinta Hill, killing the American soldiers above, and then break out of the tunnel in a banzai charge.

Nonaka found a spot in the main tunnel and waited. At thirty-two years old, he'd already served in the Imperial Navy and was surprised when he was called back to service in August 1944 as the tide of the war turned against Japan. Assigned to the 328th Naval Construction Unit, he wasn't trained to fight, but to build airfields. Yet as the Americans drove toward Manila, his unit was sent to Corregidor to create defenses to stop the expected amphibious assault. The attack came from the air instead. Nonaka had watched in awe as the paratroopers landed on Topside. A few of his unit mates opened fire with the unit's two or three Type-44 cavalry rifles, but they hit nothing. Trapped on the low ground, he joined the rest of his unit in Malinta Tunnel. Some of the soldiers and marines in the tunnel complex kept fighting, venturing out at night to ambush the Americans. But Nonaka did little fighting. His unit had only a few guns—one for every four men—and he rarely had a weapon.

When all was ready, the communication tunnel was sealed and a fuse was set. Nonaka held his breath as he and the almost 3,000 men huddled near the opening ready to attack. He heard the thunder of the explosion. The blast seemed to roll through the tunnel. The whole tunnel complex shook like an earthquake as the concussive force searched for a release. Nonaka couldn't see through the dust, debris, and smoke. He choked and gagged as he scrambled over dead bodies looking for a way out. Any order in the tunnel disintegrated into chaos as the Japanese went from a fighting force to survivors. Seconds before, all of the Japanese were ready to shout "Banzai!" but now with their last breath they called out for their mothers and shouted the names of their children.

Nonaka spotted a prick of light and clawed his way toward it. The explosion had reopened the east side of the tunnel and a group of survivors rushed toward it. As he reached the opening, Nonaka grabbed a discarded rifle and canteen and followed the others toward Kindley Landing Field on the tail of the island.

He was staggering more than walking when the cover of darkness disappeared. Overhead, flares lit up the path as the Americans, after hearing the explosion, searched for escaping Japanese. Soldiers on the hill above the tunnels shouted when they saw the survivors. Machine-gun fire followed. Nonaka crawled for cover as American bullets exploded around him. Unable to move, he waited in a hole for the flare to die, and when darkness returned, he ran toward the water's edge with a small group of survivors. American sailors on a nearby destroyer spotted them and the ship's guns opened fire. It sounded like a thunderstorm as shells smashed into the beach, sending geysers of sand and rock into the air. After the first volley, Nonaka worked his way inland toward a tunnel on the eastern section of the island. It was a hospital. Two hundred survivors made it out of the tunnel, but now they were stuck on the tail of the island. There were few guns and no ammunition. The surviving officers told the men to evacuate the island by any means possible. Those who were too injured to swim were to take their own lives. Sitting near the hospital tunnel, Nonaka stared at a tree. All of its leaves were blasted off and the bark was covered in blood. He had to get off the island.

The next night, Nonaka bundled some driftwood to use as a raft and splashed into the North Channel. He paddled for the

Bataan Peninsula using a bayonet. American ships patrolled nearby. The PT boats came close to shore, but didn't spot him. Soon, the Bataan Peninsula grew closer and closer. He was going to make it. He waded ashore and fell exhausted on the beach only to be greeted by an American patrol searching for Japanese stragglers from Corregidor. Nonaka didn't want to fight anymore. He surrendered and was sent to a POW camp.

Nonaka was one of the lucky ones.

Bradford heard the rumors that a few Japanese tried to swim the three-mile channel to Mariveles. A naval officer later confirmed it. He told Bradford that American PT boats found fifty or so swimmers a night. A few reached the opposite shore and ran off, but most got picked up by the navy or patrols onshore.

But even in deep water with no means of escape, most Japanese refused to surrender. One swimmer tried to fire at a PT boat using a carbine concealed in hollow bamboo. He got off one shot before the sailors cut him down with the boat's machine guns. Others attacked the sailors with knives. After a while, the PT boat crews just machine-gunned the Japanese and picked up their bodies the next morning in a barge.

WITH MALINTA HILL secure, the Thirty-Fourth rotated off Corregidor to join the Twenty-Fourth Infantry Division, their parent unit. Meanwhile, Colonel Jones was compressing the Japanese to the east, down the island's tail. Paratroopers were ordered toward a rocky outcropping on the south shore called Monkey Point near Kindley Field.

On the way, they found the mouth of the Navy Radio Intercept Tunnel. Often referred to as the Navy Tunnel for short, it had once housed the only American unit entirely withdrawn from Corregidor before its surrender in 1942: the cryptographers and the radio-traffic analysts who had monitored Japanese navy radio communications. The area around the tunnel was surrounded by a number of radio antenna posts.

Two companies of Japanese defenders had been spotted running into the tunnel, and a company from First Battalion moved forward to cover the entrance. A paratrooper was killed as he approached the steel doors that sealed the tunnel, so a Sherman tank was called forward with orders to blow the door off its hinges. The paratroopers were sitting or leaning against trees, taking advantage of what shade they could get from the direct sun, when the Sherman arrived, rolling down the bomb-pitted road to get into position.

A paratrooper watching the tank shook his head. He'd served with a mechanized regiment and was happy to be airborne. "Brother, there is one service that I don't want any part of," he said to a buddy as the tank rolled by. "When I wake up from bad dreams at night, there's two things I think about—one is being caught under enemy mortar fire, and the other is getting ordered to take a tank up against a fortified position."

"Well, this is one time that you can watch from the sidelines," his friend said.

"I don't even like to watch it," the man replied, and turned away from the mouth of the tunnel.

Smoke started to appear at the doorway, and the tank, now

with a direct line of fire, blasted a round into the steel doors. A split second later, a tremendous shock wave. The troops on top of the hill above the tunnel disappeared into a cloud of dust and debris. The Sherman somersaulted up in the air before crashing back to the ground upside down, killing all its crew but one. A landslide buried a platoon scouting along one side of the hill.

Even today, no one can say whether the Japanese set it off themselves, or whether the tank's round exploded the munitions in the tunnel. Either way, the sound of the blast reverberated for ten miles. A piece of rock even struck a man on Topside. When the dust cleared, a crater the width of five tennis courts and two stories deep had replaced the advancing soldiers. Bodies were strewn across the road and beach, the wounded intermingled with the dead. Some were half buried in dirt and debris. Those who weren't wounded jumped into action digging out survivors and bringing the wounded to trucks waiting to leave for Topside.

Bradford was in the aid station when he felt the violent tremor, and then heard the ear-shattering explosion. The echo was still ringing in his ears when the nearby telephone started to ring. Major Stevens, the regimental surgeon, put out a call on the radio for every doctor, medic, and corpsman in the area to go to either the scene of the explosion or the aid station. Even the destroyers offshore sent help.

"Prepare for a lot of casualties," Stevens said over the radio. "The First Battalion has been caught in a big explosion and we are sending all the trucks we can get down to pick up the wounded."

Colonel Jones sent every truck and ambulance to the scene.

He arrived at the crater shortly after the explosion and stood in silence as he looked over a field strewn with arms, legs, and blasted torsos. Some of the dead were killed by the concussion of the blast and appeared to be still alive, lying with their eyes toward the afternoon sun. The scene broke Jones's heart. So many of his men lost in an instant.

"This was by far the saddest moment of my military career," Jones wrote later. "I have more than once 'clammed up' when relating this incident. Just thinking about it still brings me grief."

CALHOUN, LIKE THE rest of Topside, felt the shock wave and heard the blast. He rushed back to the lighthouse. His men were focused on the action near the tail of the island. Some were standing on the water tanks to get a better view. Calhoun asked what happened. The men said they were cheering on the troopers advancing on the tunnel when they saw and then heard the explosion. Some of the men saw the Sherman tank get tossed into the air.

"Like a tin can tumbling end over end," one of the paratroopers told Calhoun.

A half hour after the blast, Calhoun heard trucks rumble up the road, bringing the wounded to the aid station. After the trucks started, they didn't stop. Once unloaded, they'd head back to Bottomside to get more of the wounded and later the dead.

While the wounded were evacuated, Calhoun waited for orders, first at the lighthouse and then at the company command post. He wandered over to the aid station at the barracks and watched the trucks bringing in the casualties. The men were dazed, with dried blood on their faces from bloody noses and on their necks from ruptured eardrums. Because they were unable to hear, the medics touched the men to get them to move.

The scene was too much, and Calhoun left the aid station to return to his platoon. On his way to the lighthouse, he passed an idle truck. In the back were the bodies of the dead stacked like cordwood. Bodies blown open. Missing legs. Arms. A scrotum hung between the wood extension of the sideboards.

The testicles were intact.

NYCUM HAD BEEN patrolling north of Kindley Field when he felt the explosion. Looking back, he saw a ball of dirt and smoke climb into the air. "Take cover!" someone yelled as rock and debris rained down on Nycum's patrol.

As he clambered for cover, Nycum saw logs and huge rocks tumbling down from the sky. From a crater, he watched boulders and debris crash into the seawater near a destroyer patrolling the channel between Corregidor and Bataan.

After the explosion, Nycum's company was ordered to finish clearing the area around Monkey Point. Man-made gullies built to carry rainwater to the ocean cut into the landscape. Nycum led his company off the road that wound through the area and over a culvert. As he passed in front of it, shots rang out from the culvert. Nycum hit the ground.

"Bazooka!" Nycum yelled.

The bazooka team crawled up to his location near the culvert.

"See if you can hit the corner of the culvert without exposing yourself," Nycum told them.

The gunner looked around the corner and under the road and spotted the culvert.

"Wait till I'm in position to jump into the gully," Nycum said.

The plan was to hit the culvert with a rocket and then Nycum would rush the survivors. Nycum crawled forward into the gully and gave the bazooka team a signal.

The gunner cleared the corner and fired a rocket into the mouth of the culvert. Seconds after the rocket exploded, Nycum charged forward, spraying bullets from his Thompson submachine gun.

As the echo of the Thompson faded, he saw that one of the Japanese defenders was missing the top of his head, sheared off by the bazooka rocket. A pistol hung from the neck of another soldier. Using his jump knife, Nycum cut it free and took it back to the bazooka gunner.

"Nice shot, here's a souvenir," he said, handing the pistol over.

As he climbed out of the gully, he spotted one of his unit mates near a piece of sheet metal lying against the hill. The trooper was about to pull the sheet metal away from the hole.

"Look out," Nycum said. "It may be a sniper."

The trooper took Nycum's advice and slowly approached the metal. Throwing it aside, he fell back, startled, as a Japanese soldier with a bayonet leapt out. The trooper raised his rifle and pulled the trigger.

Misfire.

Nycum and others shouldered their rifles as the Japanese soldier closed in on the stunned paratrooper. Their shots stopped him before he got to his target.

Up ahead, the Japanese had stacked fifty-five-gallon drums in a half-moon wall in front of a hill near Monkey Point. Nycum picked his way through the craters to the base of the wall. Using the barrel of his Thompson, he raised his helmet up over the lip of the wall, hoping to draw any fire.

After several seconds, Nycum moved the helmet to the left and popped his head up to the right and took a quick look. The wall covered the mouth of a large cave. Movement to his left caught his eye. Nycum ducked back down behind the barrier and took his last phosphorus grenade off his belt.

One, one thousand.

Two, one thousand.

Three, one thousand.

Nycum sent the grenade into the cave.

Smoke poured from the mouth and a lone Japanese defender came over the wall. His uniform was smoking as Nycum's unit mates shot him dead. As Nycum went to join his patrol, something bit into his right shoulder and fell at his feet. Shrapnel. He picked it up with his right hand, but when he tried to pull his arm back toward his body, pain fired through his arm. His arm just hung by his side.

"Medic!" Nycum heard a paratrooper call out as he went down to one knee.

When the medic got to Nycum, he stuck him with a morphine

syrette. Nycum's shoulder was peppered with shrapnel and the force of the blast had dislocated it. The medic stripped Nycum's shirt and immobilized his right arm with adhesive tape from his stomach to his neck.

"Do you think you can walk?" the medic shouted.

Nycum nodded, not sure why the medic was yelling at him. The medic helped him to his feet and he headed west back toward Topside.

"Nyk, how many Japs in the enclosure?" one of the paratroopers asked him as he walked away.

Nycum had no idea, but didn't want his unit mates to stumble into danger.

"Forty."

Nycum staggered back past the gully toward Malinta Hill. As he got closer to the hill, he saw dozens of white cocoons mixed in with bodies wrapped in green ponchos.

Body bags, he thought.

Then it dawned on him: *We don't bag Japanese.*

They were his fellow 503rd paratroopers killed in the Navy Tunnel blast. They were lined up to be transported off the island. The revelation hurt more than the shrapnel in his shoulder. He walked past the rows. His throat tightened. His ears rang. Tears clouded his vision. He sobbed.

"Oh God."

Nycum couldn't walk any longer. He stumbled to the ground between the rows of dead bodies. One minute, he was among his dead brothers consumed by grief. The next minute, blackness.

His mind seemed to recede like the tide, and he heard someone say, "Oh, you're awake."

Nycum rubbed his eyes. He was in a huge room with wounded men on cots all around him.

"Where am I?"

A man laughed.

"On your way home, soldier."

He'd been taken off the island on a landing craft and was on the USS *Comfort* as it sailed to Hollandia, New Guinea.

UP ON TOPSIDE, Bradford worked for hours treating the wounded and comforting the dying. When the last man was stabilized, he finally took a break. He went outside and saw Capt. Holger S. Mouritsen, a fellow surgeon with the 462nd Parachute Field Artillery Battalion, who had been standing not far from the blast at Monkey Point. For a moment both men, covered in the blood of their patients, stood in peace.

Then the surgeon looked at Bradford.

"After the blast, I went searching for survivors," Mouritsen said. "One of my own men with a tank blown over on top of him, and just his head and chest squeezed out from under it. It was like that everywhere. When I had the cases to care for, that kept me going; but after that, it was too much."

Mouritsen had immediately begun to care for the wounded, amputating a soldier's leg that was trapped under the tank.

"As soon as I got all the casualties off, I sat down on a rock and burst out crying," the surgeon told Bradford. "I couldn't stop myself and didn't even want to. I had seen more than a man could see and stay normal."

Fifty-two paratroopers gone in one blast. There were three times that many wounded. Mouritsen was awarded a Silver Star for his actions at the blast crater.

Army headquarters on Luzon and a naval headquarters radioed out with offers of aid. In less than an hour, two extra surgeons were flown to Corregidor to help. An LST (Landing Ship, Tank) with a field hospital steamed nearby ready to take on wounded.

At the aid station, two cases worried Bradford. One needed his mangled leg amputated. But his lungs had been damaged in the blast and Bradford wasn't sure he would survive surgery. Tourniquets were strapped to the injured leg and morphine was given for the pain. But two days after the blast, the leg was getting worse and had to go or the man would die.

The only solution was a guillotine amputation, meaning the limb would be cut without closing the skin. The technique was used only in emergencies. The man was put under light anesthesia and the leg was removed. Despite Bradford's best efforts, the man didn't live through the night.

The second patient was in the same situation. His leg needed to be amputated, but Bradford's fears were founded after the other man passed away. Bradford joined the other surgeons around a table at the aid station searching for a solution.

"If we only had ice, we could freeze the leg and amputate without anesthesia," one of the surgeons said. "It's a much safer amputation because the blood doesn't carry the toxins through the system when the limb is frozen."

But Bradford just shook his head. There was no ice on Corregidor. It was like asking for a snowball in hell, he thought. Then one of the navy surgeons sent to help with casualties spoke up.

"We could get ice from a destroyer, if we had any way to reach the naval base," he said.

The regimental surgeon pricked up his ears.

"Well, the colonel will give us a Cub plane to take you over there."

Two hours later, the Cub plane landed with ice. The paratrooper's leg was packed and frozen for five hours. Then, as the patient watched, the surgeons removed his leg. His blood pressure and pulse were steady during the procedure.

"Damn good to be rid of it," the man said when it was done.

The surgery was a combined effort of every asset in the theater.

"It took the Army, the Navy, and the Air Corps to save you," the navy surgeon said as he left. "We'd have called the Marines in too, but they're busy enough at Iwo Jima."

The tunnel blast was the Japanese defenders' last gasp. The cause of the explosion was undetermined. Some said it was a mass suicide timed to kill as many Americans as possible. Another theory was that ammunition and fuel stored in the tunnels had cooked off because of the American fire.

The paratroopers met little resistance afterward. On one of

the last days, Bradford was in the aid station when a paratrooper he knew well was carried in suffering from a gunshot wound. Two years before, the man had injured his knee, and Bradford had repaired it by removing cartilage. The paratrooper had returned to duty without a complaint. But just before the jump on Corregidor, he sought out Bradford with pain in his knee.

"It's not too bad, except for long patrols and heavy marching, and climbing hills," he told Bradford. "Then it kicks up so as I can't keep up with my men."

Ever the soldier, he wanted to go on the Corregidor mission so badly that he refused to go into the hospital. It was going to be his last mission, he said, a decision that proved prophetic: a Japanese sniper shot him in the chest as he led his squad in battle. He died as Bradford and the medics tried to treat his wound.

The man's death left Bradford in despair. His unit had lost 172 paratroopers, and suffered more than 600 wounded. But the hurt of losing this last man stuck with Bradford. Seeing his comrade and friend die on the table was too much. He couldn't get out of his head the fact that the man had a farm back in Iowa where his wife and two children were awaiting his return.

On that day, the war had never felt so cruel.

CHAPTER 19

Fortress Corregidor

THE HONOR GUARD, dressed at last in clean uniforms, were congregated near the flagpole on Topside. The fresh fatigues, issued to a dozen men from each 503rd platoon, had been expected, but the new boots were a surprise. Where the hell had all these pairs been during the days of shortage on Noemfoor and Mindoro?

Some two weeks after the first wave of paratroopers had dropped from a small armada of C-47s onto this Japanese-held island fortress, the fight to retake Corregidor was over, at least officially. The telltale signs of battle were everywhere. Nearby, a parachute was still caught in the snarling limbs of a tree. Mile Long Barracks was battered and pockmarked, and the countless bomb craters still gaped all over the island. But at last, the American flag would soon fly unmolested over the paratroopers who gathered around the pole, awaiting orders to fall into formation for the upcoming ceremony. Even a platoon from the Thirty-Fourth Infantry had returned to the island for the event.

Down at South Dock, which sat next to Black Beach, where the Thirty-Fourth had stormed ashore on the battle's second day, Colonel Jones waited as a flotilla of four PT boats glided gently across the water toward Corregidor's shore. Gen. Douglas Mac-Arthur was coming back to the Rock almost three years after he had been evacuated off the island in the middle of the night.

All along the road leading from the beach to Topside, paratroopers were on alert. MacArthur might be declaring the fight for Corregidor over, but in real terms it was still quite easy to get shot on Corregidor. There were numerous small actions against remnant forces.

Calhoun's platoon was set up in the Middleside section of the island. He walked up and down the road as they waited. It was impossible not to notice how the heavy bombs and naval shelling had drastically changed the landscape. Hills were smashed and crumbling. The fortress island that once protected the mouth of Manila Bay was a shell of its former self.

The day was clear, with a slight breeze. At the dock, the flotilla came to a stop and tied up, and MacArthur and eleven members of his staff filed off the boats. Gen. Walter Krueger, commander of the Sixth Army, was also in attendance. Jones met MacArthur on the dock. Dressed in his helmet and clean fatigues, his pants bloused out of the top of his jump boots, Jones was a stark contrast to MacArthur, who wore a pressed khaki shirt and matching pants, dark aviator sunglasses, and his signature "Philippine field marshal's cap," trimmed in gold.

"Well, gentlemen, it has been a long way back," MacArthur said, as much to himself as anyone else.

MacArthur led the way off the dock, negotiating the rubble from the Malinta Hill and Monkey Point explosions, toward a small convoy of jeeps. Smoke still streamed out of one of the tunnels on Malinta Hill. The paratroopers had spent the last couple of days trying to clean up the island. Unable to dig graves in the rocky soil, the paratroopers threw the Japanese corpses over the cliffs instead, but the stink of decaying bodies hung in the air. The smell was so rank during and after the battle, the sailors passing the island had to cover their noses. The paratroopers and soldiers on Corregidor quickly got used to it.

MacArthur climbed into the first jeep, with Jones in the back. The convoy's first stop was the east entrance to Malinta Tunnel. The general got out of the jeep and walked just inside the mouth of the tunnel. Nearby were the scorched bodies of two Japanese defenders, likely killed by a flamethrower.

MacArthur saw them and turned to his entourage.

"It was bad enough for us when we were here," MacArthur said. "But it has been worse for them."

The convoy took the road around Malinta Hill toward the tail and turned just past the officers' swimming beach on the north side of the island. There was a cluster of houses there for senior officers. MacArthur had lived in one of those houses after evacuating from his home in the Manila Hotel. The houses were in ruins, but the porch to one was still standing.

MacArthur climbed the porch's three steps and smiled. "Well, I'm home again."

After a few minutes, the convoy continued toward Topside. It passed the hospital, Middleside Barracks, and the theater.

Standing by the road, the paratroopers tried not to stare as Mac-Arthur passed them. When Calhoun got word the general was on Topside, he released his men from duty.

"You're free to watch the ceremony," Calhoun said.

MacArthur asked Jones to take him to Battery Wheeler, and there the old general strolled around, inspecting the ruined gunports, remembering how the once-great coastal guns had commanded the waterways around Corregidor. MacArthur knew the jagged, peculiarly shaped rock had protected Manila Bay and the city of Manila for centuries. For four decades, as MacArthur was rising from junior officer to one of the top generals in the US Army, Corregidor had been a bastion of American might in the Pacific, as formidable a fortress as any. But that fortress had failed to stop the Japanese, and three years later it failed to stop a determined Allied assault. The age of the airplane and the airborne invasion had changed warfare forever.

"Gentlemen," MacArthur said to his staff officers, "Corregidor is living proof that the day of the fixed fortress is over."

Before leaving the battery, MacArthur stood alone and looked across the South China Sea at the mountains of Bataan. Then he returned to his jeep and headed to the flagpole near the parade ground. He arrived just before noon. The men from the 503rd and the Thirty-Fourth were waiting in formation. Jones called the honor guard to attention.

The colonel stepped forward and saluted General MacArthur. "Sir, I present to you Fortress Corregidor."

MacArthur looked up at the flagpole and back at Jones.

"Colonel Jones, the capture of Corregidor is one of the most brilliant operations in military history," the general said. "Outnumbered two to one, your command by its unfaltering courage, its invincible determination, and its professional skill overcame all obstacles and annihilated the enemy. I have cited to the order of the day all units involved, and I take great pride in awarding you as their commander the Distinguished Service Cross as a symbol of the fortitude, the devotion, and the bravery with which you have fought. I see the flagpole still stands. Have your troopers hoist the colors to its peak, and let no enemy ever haul them down."

Jones executed an about-face and gave the order to present arms. Everyone saluted, and two buglers sounded "To the Colors" as Cpl. Donald Bauer, a twenty-one-year-old paratrooper from Dayton, Ohio, hoisted the flag. It snapped in the breeze as it reached the top of the pole.

Calhoun watched with a group of officers on the second-floor porch in front of Mile Long Barracks. Despite their great view, the officers paid little attention to the ceremony. To them, the real flag raising had happened on the first day, when Arrigo and Bates had climbed up the pole under fire and hung the banner for all to see. They'd fought under it, and some had died under it. They'd left and returned from patrols under it. It was their flag. This flag, MacArthur's flag, was for him and the cameras. The real flag had arrived by parachute, and once raised it never came down.

The ceremony had the opposite effect on Bradford.

He joined a friend on the top of the old barracks. Watching the ceremony gave Bradford goosebumps. He was proud of what they'd done on Corregidor, and the ceremony, while symbolic, roused a patriotism in him.

"The Japanese had first come here thinking that Americans were a 'soft' people," Bradford wrote later. "A higher civilization always acquires that reputation among barbarians. But a nation is not soft until its sons lose their willingness to risk their lives for their ideals. The paradox of Corregidor, and of the whole Pacific War for that matter, proved that the soldier who wants to live is a better fighting man than the kamikaze fanatic who is happy to die. The Americans braved death as fearlessly as the Japanese, but in a very different spirit. The bushido cult with its samurai leadership failed in this final struggle against the self-reliant discipline of the four freedoms."

There was no doubt that the ceremony christened the 503rd as the Rock Regiment. The unit's old identity of a parachuting wildcat was retired. The paratroopers of the 503rd Parachute Infantry Regiment saw themselves as the unit that took back the symbol of American might in the Pacific. Their old patch was replaced by one depicting an eagle with the shape of Corregidor Island in its talons.

When the ceremony was over, his friend turned to Bradford.

"Well, that ends the story of Corregidor, the true story," he said. "From now on it's a legend and belongs to the scenario writers. They'll make comic-strip heroes out of the real men who fought here. I'm glad we saw our part. They can have theirs."

MacArthur left the parade field and headed for the waiting PT boats. During the tour, the press corps and staff officers had ransacked the island for souvenirs. They collected parachutes, even though the paratroopers who had used them were under orders to leave them for salvage. As the dignitaries drove back to the dock with jeeps full of silk, the paratroopers seethed.

"We busted our asses jumping on this rock pile, and the rear-base commandos come out and take what they want," was the chorus from the men.

With the dignitaries gone, the paratroopers set upon the remaining parachutes. They cut them up and made skirts using the silk and suspension lines. The officers looked the other way. They couldn't enforce the order now. Later on, many of the officers' girlfriends were married in canopy silk.

Back at South Dock, the PT squadron started their engines in unison after MacArthur and his entourage climbed aboard. Jones watched from the dock. MacArthur removed his hat and placed it over his heart. Tears welled in his eyes as the boats departed.

Thank you, MacArthur mouthed in the direction of Jones.

MacArthur would later call his visit to Corregidor a moment of "drama and romance" in his life.

"We went back to The Rock the same way we had left it," MacArthur wrote in his memoir, *Reminiscences.* "We had departed in the darkness of a somber night. We came back in the sunlight of a new day. In the background, the ragged remnants of our parachutes dangled from the jagged tree stumps, the skeleton remains of the old white barracks of Topside gleamed down on us, and a smart-looking honor guard rendered us its salute."

Minutes after the general's departure, paratroopers found and killed a Japanese sniper near Malinta Hill.

———

AFTER THE CEREMONY, it was time for the 503rd to leave the island. They were moving back to Mindoro to prepare for a new mission. But before they left, Maj. Gen. G. P. Hall, Commanding General, Second Corps, came to Corregidor for a medal ceremony. Each company sent a man to receive a Silver Star medal and two to receive Bronze Star medals.

F Company selected a sergeant in the company headquarters, much to Calhoun's astonishment. While Calhoun and his men were in harm's way, the headquarters was safe inside the walls of 28-D or up on Way Hill. Private Lampman was a better candidate, but he was passed over despite firing his BAR from the hip, killing all seven Japanese holding up the advance of the platoon as they cleared Battery Boston on the first day.

Instead, narratives were written to justify each award. The only deserving soldier standing in front of Hall, in Calhoun's opinion, was Roscoe Corder, who had fought valiantly at Battery Monja, where Emory Ball was killed. The rest of the ceremony was a dog-and-pony show, he thought. A collection of stories—lies, if Calhoun was feeling impolite—to please a general. Stories that weren't worth the paper they were printed on.

NYCUM MISSED ALL the pomp and circumstance. He spent several days on the hospital ship before being transferred to a hospital in Hollandia. There, Nycum was in heaven—it was the first real mattress he'd slept on in years. On his second day at the hospital, a doctor removed his bandages and inspected his wound. It felt like a hot poker was stabbing into his shoulder.

"How did it happen, son?" the doctor asked.

Nycum shook his head. "I thought I was sunburned."

The doctor laughed.

"Someone is praying damned hard for you to come home," he said.

The wound was numbed and the doctor probed it with tweezers, finally fishing out a gray fragment and holding it up for inspection.

"It looks like a bullet," the doctor said.

After a closer look, they saw that it was a splinter of steel. The doctor checked the range of movement on Nycum's shoulder. Overhead, Nycum heard the sound of a plane engine.

"Are they ours?" the doctor asked Nycum.

While Nycum leaned to look out the window, the doctor jerked his arm and popped his shoulder back into its socket. The pain had Nycum gritting his teeth and clenching his fists, but he succeeded in playing the tough paratrooper.

Back at the hospital ward, Nycum worked the room, talking to the sailors and other soldiers recovering. For the next month, he kept track of the war and where the 503rd was while he healed. After a month, a ward attendant arrived at Nycum's bedside with his clothes, including his leggings.

"Am I being discharged?"

"No," the attendant said. "You're being sent home." He shook Nycum's hand. "Good luck."

But Nycum had no interest in going back to the United States.

He checked in with the rumor mill and found out the 503rd was headed back to Mindoro. He packed his things and got dressed and headed for the airfield.

Working his way down the flight line, Nycum hit up the crews asking where they were headed. Finally, he found a C-47 loaded with tires headed for Mindoro.

"Can I hitch a ride?" he asked.

The crew chief talked to the pilot and Nycum got the thumbs-up. Takeoff was at 0700 the next day.

"I won't be late," Nycum told the crew chief.

That night, Nycum barely slept. He was up before dawn and back at the airfield. On the flight line, he found the plane headed to Mindoro and crawled into the back. He felt at home. The C-47 was the same type of aircraft that had delivered him to Corregidor. Static-line cables ran the length of the plane. No rear door. Instead of paratroopers, tires were stacked in rows with a cable running the length to keep them together.

Half an hour before takeoff, the crew arrived. After preflight checks, they started the engines, taxied to the end of the runway, and took off. Nycum sat near the side door staring at the ocean. He couldn't contain his excitement. He'd made it.

BEFORE DAWN ON March 8, the paratroopers started their departure from Corregidor. Because there were too few trucks, Calhoun's platoon didn't head toward Bottomside until noon. The lower areas of the island were wrecked. He saw piles of concrete with rebar sticking out like pins in a cushion. Corrugated metal roofing, twisted and broken, was strewn across the ground. He even spotted smashed Springfield rifle barrels—the American defenders had destroyed the weapons before surrendering in 1942.

The paratroopers were slated to depart from the North Dock. Crowded on the beach, they killed time checking out the Shinyo suicide boats.

The LCIs arrived in pairs. By five P.M., Calhoun and his men were on board and heading out into the South China Sea. He stood near the conning tower. Painted on the tower was a straight diamond flush, ace to five. A winning hand.

But Calhoun didn't feel like a winner.

He stared back at the cliffs of Topside as the sun slipped under the western horizon. He felt like he was on the edge of a dark hole, his mind on the verge of collapse. He struggled to remember his friends. His fellow officers like Ball and Flash. His men, who died under his orders. His mind drifted to the bodies shrouded in mattress covers turned into body bags. Each one closed with a bow.

How many times were we survivors near death and never realizing it? he thought.

As the island slipped away, the weight of what he'd just survived caught up with him. He should have been happy. Mission accomplished. He'd survived a brutal fight. One that tried to take his life and his humanity.

But many of his friends were leaving maimed or dead. They had given up their own hopes and dreams to protect their nation. None chose death. All loved life as much as Calhoun. But they knew the minute they jumped into the wind or stepped onto the beach there was no escaping their fate.

Calhoun stood in silence watching the island slip away. He felt nothing but grief. He'd left too many souls on Corregidor.

The price of victory was steep.

EPILOGUE

Homeward Bound

THE 503RD'S WAR wasn't over after Corregidor.

When the paratroopers got back to Mindoro, they were put on alert for another combat jump, this time in the central Philippines to reinforce the Fortieth Infantry Division on Negros Island.

Before leaving Mindoro, Calhoun was appointed F Company summary courts officer to handle the personal effects of the deceased. Efforts to change George Mikel's beneficiary hit a stone wall, but he did send Betty, Mikel's Australian wife, his camera and the money from his fatigues. When he never heard from Betty, Calhoun was sure the letter never arrived. But decades later, Calhoun discovered that it did get all the way back to her in Australia.

He'd kept his word.

The Negros jump was canceled, but the mission was not. In April 1945, the 503rd, including both Nycum and Lopez, hit the beach aboard LCIs and spent the rest of the war patrolling the island's jungle, mopping up Japanese soldiers who fought with the same fanatical zeal as the defenders of Corregidor. The paratroopers were undersupplied and poorly led. The regiment even had to paste aerial photos together to create maps. The Japanese consistently had the upper hand despite rumors that they were a beaten force.

Then, on August 6 and 9, 1945, the United States detonated two nuclear bombs over the Japanese cities of Hiroshima and Nagasaki. Over 6,150 Japanese soldiers soon surrendered to the 503rd, although the whole force on Negros didn't submit until October. On September 2, 1945, General MacArthur broadcast a speech from the deck of the USS *Missouri* in Tokyo Harbor. The Pacific war was over.

Three months after MacArthur's message, eighteen Japanese stragglers emerged from the jungle on Corregidor. They surrendered to a lone American soldier marking the location of American graves on the island. The Japanese had been hiding in an underground tunnel and learned the war was over only when they found a newspaper announcing the surrender while searching for water.

The battle for Corregidor cost 228 American lives, with another 727 wounded or injured. Japanese casualties were steep: 4,497 Japanese died defending the island. And 119 Japanese were taken prisoner.

Five Americans died for every one hundred Japanese.

Unlike the larger airborne operations in Europe, the 503rd had been forced to perform with more precision than any other parachute unit during World War II. The jump was made under tough conditions. The landing zone was small, and the jumpers faced strong winds and heavy enemy resistance. But the surprise attack resulted in the immediate possession of Topside, the heart of the Japanese defense. Aggressive patrolling and decisive action allowed the 3,000 paratroopers, reinforced by 1,000 infantrymen, to completely wipe out a defending force of about 6,500 Japanese.

As with any victory, the paratroopers were lucky. Instead of finding a gap in the line—and there were many—Endo attacked strongpoints on Wheeler Point and Calhoun's position on Battery Hearn. Commanders also turned off the radio net. Had they kept the radio net up, the paratroopers could have called for fire from the ships patrolling the island. Calhoun wrote later that he believed "good men died from poor command decisions."

But now the war was over, and the 503rd paratroopers were finally headed home. Most of the men returned to civilian life. Some better than others.

Soon after the 503rd arrived on Negros Island, orders came to take Lloyd McCarter out of action immediately. McCarter was still wounded and convalescing in a military hospital. When he awoke from surgery, a military policeman was standing guard in the recovery ward.

"Good God, what have I done now?" McCarter said.

But the guard was there to watch several wounded Japanese being treated by American doctors.

The awards board agreed with Calhoun that McCarter deserved at least a Distinguished Service Cross, the second-highest award for valor. But the board's unanimous opinion was that McCarter deserved the Congressional Medal of Honor. Calhoun provided a map, a description of the weather and light conditions, and two sworn statements from Second Lt. John Mara and Tech. Sgt. Philip Todd.

McCarter was sent to a hospital in San Francisco, where he received a letter from President Harry Truman. It was an invitation to the White House. On September 10, 1945, Truman personally awarded him the Congressional Medal of Honor.

McCarter was discharged later that year. He married and lived a quiet life but fell into a deep depression after his wife died due to cancer. He was also in great pain from his war wounds, which had left a bullet in his body close to his heart that surgeons couldn't remove.

On February 2, 1956, McCarter took his own life with a single gunshot. He was only thirty-eight years old.

Charlie Bradford returned to his medical practice in Boston and was active in the Massachusetts National Guard. He was an orthopedic surgeon at Boston City Hospital until his retirement in the 1970s. Bradford died of a heart attack at Jordan Hospital in Plymouth, Massachusetts, in May 2000. He was ninety-five.

Chet Nycum got back to the 503rd just in time. After four months fighting in the jungle in Negros, he was sent home. He handed over his Thompson submachine gun and a .38-caliber pistol to his replacement and boarded a truck that took him to a waiting ship back to his wife, Margaret.

They stayed married for the next sixty-eight years. Nycum

worked at USE Westinghouse Electric Corporation overseeing testing and evaluating radar systems for the next three decades. Pieces of shrapnel continued to find their way to the surface of his back until the mid-1950s, and memories of his dead friends and the enemies he killed lived in his dreams the rest of his life.

Nycum died in September 2013. He was ninety-two.

After passing out from his gunshot wound, Anthony Lopez woke in a bed near the window in the aid station on Corregidor with no recollection of how he got there. Five days later, he was evacuated with other wounded to a hospital ship and then an army hospital in Leyte. He was shocked when he was awarded the Purple Heart while still convalescing.

"What for?" he said. "I'm just doing what everyone else is doing."

Instead of going home, he remained in the hospital for two weeks before he was reunited with the 503rd in Mindoro and continued to fight until the Japanese surrender.

After the war, Lopez was sent home, arriving back in the United States in December 1945. He reenlisted into the Eighty-Second Airborne Division and got married, having two sons and a daughter. Lopez left the army for good five years later and went back to Denver, where he went to school with the help of the GI Bill and later became a mechanic. He owned a transmission repair shop for fifty years.

I met Lopez in 2018 at his home in Denver. We sat at his kitchen table and he told me his story. In his nineties, his memory was spotty but he told the story to the best of his recollection. It was riveting. But like all combat veterans, he wanted to talk about his friends and the funny stuff, like stealing trucks or making apple pies, more than what he did in the ravine.

He did tell the story about a brace of .38 revolvers he had received in exchange for a brass-knuckle trench knife. Lopez was on his way to relieve a buddy on guard duty when his friend Charlie Stewart picked up the revolvers and started to twirl them like the Hollywood cowboys.

"Careful," Lopez said. "They've got a hair trigger."

Stewart laughed off the warning. "That's OK because I'm a cowboy at heart."

Seconds later, as Stewart went to spin one of the revolvers into the holster on his belt, the gun went off. The bullet hit Stewart in the right calf.

Lopez shook his head and took the guns away.

"See," he said. "And you won't even get a Purple Heart."

Lopez was still chuckling in 2018 as he recalled the story. The more I talked with him, the more I saw what I've seen from soldiers in Iraq and Afghanistan. The terror of combat was better left in the past. The best stories were the ones that happened in the quiet moments, especially if they ended with a laugh.

But one thing he made very clear. He wasn't a hero, even when he went down into the ravine.

"I have been called a hero many times," Lopez wrote in a short memoir of his time in the 503rd. "But I tell them, I am not a hero. I went through World War II and had my wounds but I came home. I married, raised a family and lived a full life. My heroes are my friends and brothers who at the age of eighteen, nineteen and twenty years old never had that opportunity. Their lives taken from them before they were grown up . . . Those that never came home, never saw their families or friends, those in my opinion are the true heroes."

The last time I heard from Yolanda, Lopez's daughter, he was on oxygen and doing home hospice. We planned on co-hosting a book signing in Denver in 2020, but Lopez passed away September 5, 2019. He was laid to rest at Fort Logan National Cemetery on September 16, 2019. He was ninety-four years old.

After the war, Bill Calhoun went back to school. He attended Tarleton State College and graduated from the University of Texas in 1948. In 1952 he graduated from Baylor Dental School and opened Calhoun's Dental Office in Comanche, Texas. Calhoun was a member of First Baptist Church of Comanche, where he served as a lifetime deacon and taught Sunday school. He also served more than two decades in the National Guard, retiring as a colonel. He and Sarah Joe had two daughters. Sarah Joe passed away in 2007.

Calhoun, at the age of ninety-two, died on November 22, 2014, in Comanche, almost seven decades after he left the Philippines for home at the end of the war. It was a journey home that he almost hadn't survived. Relieved of command in Negros on October 17, 1945, he soon reported to a camp on Leyte, where he finally boarded a ship headed for San Francisco on November 23. The USS *Cape Bon* was the slowest and sorriest ship in the US service, in Calhoun's opinion. For three days, it was pounded by the edge of a typhoon, during which the screeching and moaning of the steel hull made it seem that the ship was coming apart. The rudder became damaged by the storm, forcing the ship to slow down even more to keep from losing it.

A day out of San Francisco, the ship was ordered to Portland, Oregon, due to overcrowding in the port. Calhoun was finally back in the United States when the ship entered the Columbia River on December 18. He stood on deck and took in the farms and highways. It was joyful to behold. They docked in Portland shortly after dark and Calhoun hit US soil for the first time in almost two years. He had gone overseas on the fastest liner and came home on the slowest.

All returning soldiers were sent to Fort Lewis and were greeted with a steak dinner with all the fixings. To Calhoun, eating fresh lettuce was the real treat. He hadn't had it in years. The next morning, he tried to call Sarah Joe, but didn't have any luck. The lines were jammed with thousands of similar calls.

After processing at Fort Lewis, he was on a train to Texas. He got to Fort Bliss on December 22 and boarded the final train home. Calhoun was at the door of Sarah Joe's parents' house at dawn, Christmas Eve.

When Sarah Joe appeared, all was right in the world.

A Note on the Sources

THE BULK OF the narrative was constructed using three unpublished manuscripts written by Bradford, Calhoun, and Lopez. I also used oral histories from the National Museum of the Pacific War in Fredericksburg, Texas, and from the 503rd Heritage Battalion, and an in-person interview with Lopez in Denver in 2018.

Calhoun's family provided a copy of his memoir—much of it printed out by a dot-matrix printer with handwritten edits—and Paul F. Whitman provided me with an edited copy with added context. Whitman also provided a copy of Bradford's book *Combat over Corregidor*. The book offered Bradford's recollections of the battle. The manuscript was a key source for previous authors on this subject, such as Gerard M. Devlin's *Back to Corregidor: America Retakes the Rock* and *Corregidor: The Rock Force Assault* by Gen. E. M. Flanagan. Both books were also used as a reference.

Dan King found and translated Yoshiharu Nonaka's recollections of his time on Corregidor, which provided at least a glimpse of the battle from the Japanese perspective.

Finally, Whitman's treasure trove of pictures and documents on his website, http://www.corregidor.org, was invaluable. His collection is unsurpassed and a real treasure for anyone interested in Corregidor or the 503rd Parachute Infantry Regiment.

Acknowledgments

NO BOOK IS written in a vacuum. So many people helped make this project a reality.

Todd Mayer put me on the right track. He was instrumental in helping me find sources and helped me get my arms around the battle. Dennis Blocker started the research process for me and was a huge help in tracking down sources of information. If you're looking for a researcher—especially about the Pacific war—there are few I'd recommend more than him.

Dan King—a renowned researcher and author of the Japanese perspective of the Pacific war—helped me search for Japanese sources and educated me about the Japanese Imperial military. King tried to find Japanese narratives of the battle, but found very little. He did uncover Yoshiharu Nonaka's statement about his service on Corregidor. While short, its retelling of the Malinta Hill explosion was invaluable and brought a glimpse into the Japanese side of the battle to this story. Lauren Robertson allowed me to use a rare photo of her grandfather with Bradford.

Kelly Taylor, one of Calhoun's daughters, invited me into her home and let me rummage through her father's papers. She also trusted me with a copy of his memoirs. My one regret is never having had the chance to meet Calhoun in person. I hope I did his story justice.

No one suffered more than Becky Grogan and Mitch Weiss, who were forced to read early drafts. Their insight was instrumental in improving the manuscript.

Thanks to Frank Weimann, my agent, for making this whole thing possible. He believed in the idea and helped make it a reality.

Thanks also to Brent Howard, John Parsley, Christine Ball, and Amanda Walker at Dutton for taking on this book with me. They are the best team in publishing and this book is better because of their hard work, especially Brent, whose edits helped shape and improve this story immeasurably. This is as much his book as it is mine. If you like the book, thank Brent.

Paul F. Whitman, historian and tour guide extraordinaire, and John Moffitt took me to Corregidor in 2019 and made sure I saw every important place on the island. Thank you both for the long walks and insight into the battle and the Philippines. It is a trip I'll never forget.

An extra thanks to Whitman who, like Becky and Mitch, read early drafts and helped fact-check the manuscript. His edits kept me out of trouble and made each page better. There are few men around who know the history of Corregidor better than Whitman. The book would not exist without his help and generosity. But any mistakes are mine alone.

Finally, thank you to my family for putting up with me as I struggled to tell this story and for understanding when the book came first. This project was temporary; you're forever.

Index

Index

Browning Automatic Rifle (BAR)
  and airborne assault of Corregidor,
    81–82
  and attack on Batteries Smith and
    Hearn, 165, 167
  and attack on Battery Monja, 217
  and attack on Battery Wheeler, 95–96
  and defense of Cheney Ravine, 117
  and hand-to-hand combat, 234
  and Japanese attacks on Topside,
    106–9, 173, 178–80
  and Lampman's heroics, 95–96, 258
  and patrol of Grubbs Ravine, 208
  and preparations for invasion,
    48–49, 54
Buchanan, Henry L., 221, 225–26,
  228, 230
Bugsanga River, 15, 58
bureaucracy of the military, 232–33
bushido cult, 256

C-47 Skytrain transports
  and airborne assault of Corregidor, 59,
    61–63, 69, 75, 77–80
  and antiaircraft fire, 94
  and missed jumps of paratroopers,
    150–51
  and Noemfoor jump, 12
  and Nycum's return to the 503rd, 260
  preparations for invasion, 35–36, 51
  and resupply missions, 127
Caballo Island, xiv, 132
Calhoun, Bill
  action at Noemfoor, 13–14
  action prior to Corregidor, 9–11
  administrative duties, 232
  airborne assault of Corregidor, 75–80,
    82–86
  award recommendations, 233–34,
    265–66
  background, 46–48
  at Batteries Smith and Hearn, 157–61,
    163–68, 163–69, 213–14
  at Battery Wheeler, 89–95, 95–105,
    138–49
  ceremony for recapture of Corregidor,
    252, 254–55
  at Corregidor lighthouse, 195–96

criticisms of command at
  Corregidor, 265
departure from Corregidor, 260–62
and explosion at Navy Tunnel, 242–43
firefight at Mile Long Barracks, 135
at Grubbs Ravine, 199–200, 202–8
and Japanese attacks on Topside,
  107–8, 113–14, 171–76, 177–79,
  182–83, 184–88, 189–90, 223
and Japanese snipers, 137
and looting among military units,
  17–19
marriage, 53–54, 210
medal ceremony on Corregidor, 258
on Mindoro prior to invasion,
  9–11, 15
postwar life, 269–70
preparations for invasion, 34–35, 37,
  40–46, 51, 53–54, 56
and psychological impact of battle,
  210–11
and rescue mission in Cheney Ravine,
  120–21
and souvenirs found on
  Corregidor, 233
as summary courts officer, 263
and water supplies, 193–94
at Way Hill, 191–93, 196–99
Calhoun, Sarah Joe, 53, 210, 269–70
Campbell, William, 139–42, 189
Camp Mackall, North Carolina, 53
USS *Cape Bon*, 269
carabao, 24–26
Caskey, Lawson, 32–35, 106, 222
casualties
  and airborne assault of Corregidor,
    73–74
  at Battery Hearn, 196
  at Battery Wheeler, 118, 205–6
  body counts, 196
  doctor killed during jump, 91, 94
  evacuation missions, 130–32
  and explosion at Navy Tunnel,
    241–43, 246–47
  in F Company, 195, 210
  and flies, 115–16
  injuries in airborne assault, 30, 36,
    70–71, 73–74, 86, 151

277

Index

Index

Index

Index

About the Author

Kevin Maurer is an award-winning journalist and the bestselling coauthor, with Mark Owen, of *No Easy Day: The Firsthand Account of the Mission That Killed Osama bin Laden*; *No Hero: The Evolution of a Navy SEAL*; and, with Tamer Elnoury, *American Radical: Inside the World of an Undercover Muslim FBI Agent*. He has covered the military—particularly the airborne and special operations forces—for seventeen years, including embeds in Afghanistan, Iraq, Haiti, and east and central Africa. He lives in North Carolina.